JOSEPH FARLBUSCH

541-4611

TIME-OUT LEADERSHIP

TIME-OUT LEADERSHIP

DAILY REFLECTIONS TO MAXIMIZE YOUR LEADERSHIP EFFECTIVENESS

DONALD LUCE

Thomas Nelson Publishers
Nashville • Atlanta • London • Vancouver

Published in Nashville, Tennessee, by Thomas Nelson, Inc., Publishers, and distributed in Canada by Word Communications, Ltd., Richmond, British Columbia, and in the United Kingdom by Word (UK), Ltd., Milton Keynes, England.

Unless otherwise noted, Scripture quotations are from the NEW KING JAMES VERSION of the Bible. Copyright © 1979, 1980, 1982, Thomas Nelson, Inc., Publishers. Scripture quotations noted KJV are from the King James Version of the Holy Bible.

Library of Congress Cataloging-in-Publication Data

Luce, Donald, 1958–
   Time-out leadership : daily reflections to maximize your leadership
effectiveness / Donald Luce.
      p.   cm.
   Includes bibliographical references.
   ISBN 0-7852-7565-7 (hc)
   1. Management—Quotations, maxims, etc.   2. Leadership—Quotations,
maxims, etc.   I. Title.
HD57.7.L82   1996
658.4'092—dc20   95–40762
                                                                      CIP

Printed in the United States of America
1 2 3 4 5 6 7 — 02 01 00 99 98 97 96

"Little girls are the nicest things that happen to people."

ALLAN BECK

FOR

Alexandra Grace

The nicest thing that has happened to her mother and me.

ACKNOWLEDGMENTS

There is no question that writing a book is a true labor of love. So much of oneself goes into the words on the pages. Correspondingly, so much is received from people who help to bring the words from the pages to the world.

I would like to thank the entire team at Thomas Nelson for their efforts to work around the unanticipated time frames and deadlines associated with this book. Specific appreciation is due to acquisitions editor Lonnie Hull DuPont, whose support and encouragement made this book possible, and editor Sheryl Taylor, whose upbeat, can-do spirit would be the envy of any author.

Thanks to Paul Schadler, whose words of inspiration and faith kept me focused.

Mostly, my gratitude flows to my wife, Diane. She encourages my dreams and puts up with my odd hours and travel schedule. Her unconditional love is my motivation. Every day I realize how lucky I am that we found each other.

[handwritten notes]

2,

please use for bracketing?

What is important
what do I believe
what do I practice

INTRODUCTION

"The best thinking has been done in solitude. The worst has been done in turmoil."

THOMAS ALVA EDISON

These are challenging times for leaders. The pace of the world has sped up by unthinkable proportions. Everything seems to be changing. Competition for customers and resources is at an all-time high. Globalization, once applicable to a handful of organizations, is now part of our everyday lives. We are bombarded with so much information, we cannot possibly digest it all.

Good leaders realize that with so much going on it helps to take a step back periodically and focus on direction, vision, and values. The leading experts of the day, from Stephen Covey to M. Scott Peck, encourage us to do so. In *The Fifth Discipline,* Peter Senge advises leaders that "whether it is through contemplative prayer or other methods of simply 'quieting' the conscious mind, regular meditative practice can be extremely helpful in working more productively."

Daily reflection, meditation, or contemplative prayer (whatever you want to call it) is a tool that the leader of today must master. We must be able to process the information we are receiving. We need to check out of the hub-bub for a little while and think. What is important? Where am I going? Where am I taking those who are following?

But how? Leaders tend to be practical people. There are things to do. There are fires to be put out. There are no instruction manuals on how to reflect.

Some leaders read sections of religious writings for inspiration.

Some listen to classical music. I like quotations. I spend time thinking about the words of other great leaders and their impact on me. Many years ago I started collecting quotations of great leaders. I wanted to share them with other leaders in a format that allows for thinking about the meaning behind the words.

I wrote this book to address the opportunity of reflection. I wanted to create an easy way for leaders to take time out and reflect on meaningful issues. The book is easy to use. There is a quotation for each day of the year. Below each quotation is a short reading with some of my thoughts, followed by an affirmation statement.

I find it helpful to dedicate a time each day to read that day's quotation. You may want to read the day's selection and remember and think about the quotation or the affirmation statement throughout the day, whenever the opportunity arises. As part of my daily reflection, I spend five to ten minutes of quiet time each day with these quotations. I make sure that I will not be disturbed by phones or other people. I keep a pen and paper handy to jot down any ideas that come into my head.

These quotations remind me to focus on the principles leaders need to live by in order to be successful and to help those around them develop and prosper. Five to ten minutes daily is a manageable amount of time. You may be surprised that the return of ideas and inspiration is so great.

This book is not dated. There is no specific year that it must be read. If you forget a day, you can read it another time or go on to the current day. You may just flip through the pages until a meaningful passage strikes your interest. The most important thing is to relax and enjoy.

Being a leader today is fraught with challenges. With time and thought, you have the ability to surpass all challenges and move always toward success. My best wishes. I hope this guide becomes an essential part of your daily routine.

DAY 1

———○———

"That moment when one finally commits
oneself, then Providence moves too."

GOETHE

*F*requently we begin a project or a new habit with the best intention of complete commitment. Then things get in the way, and suddenly we are no longer on the path of our original intentions. Deciding to commit is easy. The difficulty lies in living up to a commitment for the long term. This difficulty may actually cause some people to become skeptical and avoid any new commitments.

As a leader, you will find it hard to make anything happen without true personal commitment. The people who can help you make things happen may sense when you are not committed. With true commitment, whether to a project, career, or relationship, the earth moves. Opportunities present themselves when you least expect them. You will find that people are willing to work with you, even if they are not consciously aware they are doing it. Making true personal commitment with a resolution to see it through is one of the foundations of leadership excellence.

God –
family –
church –

I will focus on where in my life I need to make true commitment. By making commitments, opportunities will continually flow in my direction.

DAY
2

---○---

"There are risks and costs to a program of action,
but they are far less than the long-range risks
and costs of comfortable inaction."
JOHN F. KENNEDY

*M*any business environments make it difficult to take
risks. Taking risks can lead to huge rewards, yet
everyone knows of people who were punished for taking risks
that resulted in bad consequences. Leaders must teach others
how to calculate the risks associated with decisions and provide
the openness to discuss opportunities and challenges. The business environment is changing so quickly that inaction based on
fear, comfort zones, or organizational hierarchy can be debilitating.

Taking risks can be dangerous, but a bigger danger lies in
avoiding risk for fear of retribution. Encourage those who are
important to your success to take risks. Help them take the
necessary risks to move the organization toward a prosperous
future.

Beginning today, I will encourage more openness and risk
taking in my organization, starting with my own
actions as well as those of my associates.

DAY 3

---○---

"Integrity without knowledge is weak and useless, and knowledge without integrity is dangerous and dreadful."
SAMUEL JOHNSON

*A*s we move farther into the information age, leaders must deal in a new principal currency: knowledge. The knowledge that a leader possesses is integral to the success of those being led. We must find new ways to reward the knowledge possessed by those with whom we work. Still, a leader must not only reward and recognize knowledge; a leader must also be sure to value integrity.

To have free-flowing information, which is imperative to success, there must be trust. Leaders must demonstrate high levels of personal integrity and reward it in others so that everyone will be comfortable sharing the information necessary to complete tasks. We are in a new time. True winners not only will possess more knowledge than the competition, but also will be able to trust that this information is handled with a high level of integrity in all cases.

Today I will focus on the knowledge I can share with others to help them become more effective. I will find new ways to reward the knowledge and integrity of those around me.

DAY 4

---○---

"Every man is in some way my superior,
in that I can learn of him."
RALPH WALDO EMERSON

*L*eaders have traditionally been rewarded for their abilities to solve problems, put out fires, or move obstacles to get things done. They are the experts in their field. It feels good to solve problems and be seen as an authority. Yet it is easy to become jaded and think there is nothing new we can learn about a certain topic or process.

With all the change that is occurring in our world, we have to look for new links to understand our situations. If a leader has an air of superiority, then others may not feel an openness to share specific knowledge with that leader. We must be open to the distinct perceptions that everyone has, whether a colleague, associate, or the person on the street. Trends come from the outside in, not the inside out.

I will be open today to what I can learn
from everyone who crosses my path.

DAY
5

---

*"My theology is not a theology of believing.
My theology is a theology of doing."*
REV. CECIL WILLIAMS

*I*t can be so easy to espouse the latest theory or latest development yet not change your behavior in a significant way, even if you believe the theory with all your heart. A "do as I say, not as I do" attitude is transparent to everyone around us. It is the kind of attitude that diminishes our credibility and our ability to lead.

Why not just "do it" then, if we believe it? The answer lies in the level of energy and commitment necessary to move belief to action. Leaders must dedicate energy to do what we believe. Persuading others to do what we believe does not work unless we do it ourselves. Dedicate yourself to doing.

*Today I will focus on living my beliefs; my personal integrity
is at stake. When others see me doing what I believe
to be right, they will be inspired by my action.*

DAY
6

———○———

"If you have a company with itsy-bitsy vision,
you have an itsy-bitsy company."
ANITA RODDICK

*P*hone calls must be made. Decisions are pending. Information comes from all directions. It is easy to become so involved in our day-to-day goals that we find it difficult to focus on the big picture. Besides, with all the information coming our way, what should the big picture look like anyway?

Those we lead look to us for vision. They want a reason to work and exist. The more powerful, more encompassing, and more exciting we can make our vision, the more likely it is that those around us will be eager to help us make it happen.

What makes the work worth it? It is vision that motivates. See where you are going. Communicate where you are going. Jump to the front of the line and march into the future with all the excitement and energy you can muster.

People want to follow my vision. Today I will focus on clarifying
what the destination is and communicating it to those
who are relying on me to lead them there.

DAY 7

"Dictators ride to and fro upon tigers which they dare not dismount. And the tigers are getting hungry."
WINSTON CHURCHILL

*T*here was a time when leaders needed only to tell someone what, when, and how—and their orders were followed without a question. Leaders were all powerful. But even benevolent dictatorships eventually fall, and it is impossible to lead without the support and knowledge of loyal followers. Leaders must rely on the expertise of those around us. Yet sometimes it is easy to expect them to jump at our command without knowing the why.

If the why is compelling enough, people will struggle through almost any what, when, and how. They will support the leader who gives them their humanity, respects their abilities, and provides them with a vision. Leaders once were all-powerful. Now they must be all-empowering.

My ability to lead hinges on my ability to motivate those around me. Today I will find ways to communicate my respect for their humanity and abilities.

DAY 8

---

*"Thou art snared with the words of thy mouth,
thou art taken with the words of thy mouth."*
PROVERBS 6:2 KJV

*H*ow often do you take time to listen to what you are actually saying? What words and phrases do you use when talking about the challenges and possibilities you face? Negativity breeds negativity. Positivity breeds positivity.

A leader takes all possible steps to be sure to present a positive edge when talking to others, about others, or to oneself. You do this more for yourself than in anticipation of the positive or negative consequences your words will have for others. You move in the direction of your thoughts and speech. Be sure it is the direction in which you want others to follow you.

*Today I will listen carefully to myself. I will honestly evaluate
the impact of what I say upon others and myself.*

DAY
9

*H*ow often are we knocked down for our ideas or while following our dreams? We can take a lesson from children. When they first learn to walk, they take a series of falls. Not just one fall, but hundreds. Eventually they learn to walk.

That is what life is all about. Sometimes the accomplishment is just one more try away. Perhaps, like children, each time we are knocked down, we can get up a little quicker and stay up a little longer. Eventually we can focus on more than walking. Running, maybe, or winning races. If you have a dream, if you know it is possible, keep on trying. Victory may be one more try away.

Where have I been knocked down one too many times and given up trying? Today I will take action to persevere, and I will eventually master the opportunity.

DAY 10

"Why reach for the moon when you have the stars?"
BETTE DAVIS IN *NOW, VOYAGER*

*A*re your goals high enough? Are your aspirations on a par with your abilities? Is your vision exciting enough to move others to action?

Many of the accomplishments that seemed like science fiction only a few years ago have become part of our everyday lives. Can you set your sights higher? The path may be uncharted. It may not feel as safe as staying right where you are. The voyage for you as a leader and for those you lead will be more exciting. We are a people who thrive on discovery and adventure. Build adventure and challenge into your vision.

Today I will evaluate where I am going and set my sights a little higher. Wherever the destination, I pledge to bring a sense of adventure to all who are participating in the journey.

DAY 11

---○---

*"I do not believe in circumstances. The people who get
on in this world are the people who get up and look
for the circumstances they want, and, if they
cannot find them, make them."*
GEORGE BERNARD SHAW

*T*ime passes so quickly it is sometimes hard to remember that we need to take time to create our future and plan our path. Fires pop up randomly and need to be extinguished. Phones, faxes, electronic mail, and all the other paraphernalia of our technological society designed to save us time really take more control of it. We begin to think that things just happen to us when in reality we can create our current situation and our future.

We have the control we need to choose which circumstances we keep, which we overcome, and which we create. It takes planning. It takes action. Mostly it means that we have to make decisions about our present and future and how we want them to be. Then we must take action to assure that plan succeeds.

*I am able to control in a positive manner
which circumstances affect my life
and my ability to lead.*

DAY 12

"Tell me, I'll forget. Show me, I may remember.
But involve me and I'll understand."
CHINESE PROVERB

*H*ow often do you become frustrated with someone's lack of ability to catch on? Things are so easy for you, especially if you have been doing them for a long time. You are in a special position of leadership because of your abilities. When things are easy, it may be hard to remember that you were once in the position of learning a new skill.

There is always a learning curve. Even in an area where you had a special talent, it took time to learn. Most likely, you learned by doing. The people you lead need to learn by doing also, and they may make mistakes along the way. However, if you involve them in the process, you will increase the chances that they will learn more quickly and capture the skill more effectively. You need patience and a willingness to allow others to make mistakes.

Today I will focus on areas where I can help others learn by getting
them more involved. I have the patience and understanding
to help them through the learning curve.

DAY 13

*"It's a funny thing about life, if you refuse to accept
anything but the best, you very often get it."*
W. SOMERSET MAUGHAM

*W*hat is it that some leaders and organizations have
that attracts so much excellence? More often than
not it is an attitude. People will live up or down to your expectations of them. If much is expected and you communicate it,
people will try their hardest to achieve what you believe they can.
This is not to say that some will not try to take the path of
least resistance, but fewer will be able to if you establish clear
expectations for excellence.

The key to inspiring others to excellence is to strive for nothing
less yourself. Your integrity here is what counts the most. If those
you lead sense even the least amount of inequity between your
expectations of them and of yourself, they will gravitate toward
the lowest common denominator. Expect only the best from
others, and strive for it with your own actions.

*Today I will strive for only the best in all of
my endeavors while motivating others to do
the same through my actions and words.*

DAY 14

"We need every human gift and cannot afford to neglect any gift because of artificial barriers of sex or race or class or national origin."
MARGARET MEAD

*O*ur lives are becoming more and more diversified and internationally connected. Civil rights programs have played a part, but they are not the whole story. Free-trade agreements are opening new opportunities and challenges for leaders in the private and public sectors. Information flows freely across boundaries. Products are no longer manufactured in one place; the components are multinational.

With boundaries between nations falling at an astounding pace, it is interesting that personal boundaries and boundaries within workplaces still exist. People continually separate themselves by gender, race, nationality, and workplace status, which stifles communication and creativity. These personal and professional boundaries must continue to fall for us to be successful in our multidimensional world.

I continually examine where in my life boundaries exist that exclude others. I will take steps today to encourage more diversity in my life and in my organization.

DAY 15

---○---

*"You have not converted a man because
you have silenced him."*

JOHN MORLEY

*S*uccessful leaders possess excellent persuasion skills. There
are two kinds of persuasion, positional and participatory.
Leaders who use their workplace status to convince others of a
course of action are using positional persuasion techniques.
Leaders who gain the cooperation of others by asking questions,
finding out motivations, and asking for advice are using participatory persuasion techniques.

A lone dissenter on an issue can make it appealing to use
positional persuasion to dictate decisions. It seems like a quick
way to handle the issue, and the dissenter cannot argue anymore.
Unfortunately, dissenters do not always buy in and may consciously or unconsciously sabotage the decision. A far more effective method is to take time to talk about the issue, find out
everyone's needs, and sell them on the benefits of the plan.
Gaining their participation will help you sell your idea.

*Today I will examine areas where I need to employ exceptional
persuasion skills and concentrate on using participatory
persuasion techniques in those circumstances.*

DAY 16

---○---

"Those who decide to use leisure as a means of mental development, who love good music, good books, good pictures, good plays, good company, good conversation—what are they? They are the happiest people in the world."
WILLIAM LYON PHELPS

*A*ll too often leisure takes a backseat to work. We are responsible for so many people, for so much money, and for so much production. Leaders thrive on taking on more and more responsibility. It is hard to turn it all off, even when we are not working. Mentally we tend to still focus on the task left undone, even when the task is at the office and we are away.

Leisure pursuits help leaders put problems into the subconscious mind. The subconscious then works silently on the problems until it identifies possible solutions. In the meantime, your conscious mind gets a well-deserved break. Your body gets a chance to relax. Your personhood opens up to a positive change in perspective that allows you to see opportunities and look at problems in a whole new light.

Today I will plan more leisure into my life, which will give me a new, more balanced, and energized perspective on my work.

DAY
17

*"Once a human being has arrived on this earth,
communication is the largest single factor determining
what kinds of relationships he makes with others and
what happens to him in the world about him."*
VIRGINIA SATIR

Nothing happens in a leader's world without effective communication. Others draw conclusions about our intelligence, integrity, and credibility based on how we communicate. Our ability to be heard effectively regulates our ability to attract all those we need to be successful in our personal and organizational goals.

Part of the challenge is that everyone needs to hear our message in a unique way. We must always be sensitive to those around us and how they need communication structured. We have to determine quickly each person's individual personality style and then structure our tone and form of delivery to be heard most effectively. Even though the basic message is the same, we communicate in a different way in every circumstance.

*I will make a special effort to consciously structure
my communication with a focus on individual
needs and styles. As a result, I am able
to gain cooperation at all levels.*

DAY 18

"Education makes a people easy to lead, but difficult to drive; easy to govern, but impossible to enslave."
LORD BROUGHAM

*A*s organizations become more learning focused, leadership styles will have to continually evolve in response. It is no longer possible for the leader to hold all the information. Leaders must trust that those around them have the skills to manipulate the information at their disposal. If they do not have the skills, leaders must find ways to help those around them develop.

The new leader will continue to be responsible for the "what," but will no longer focus independently on the "how." The "how" becomes a joint venture between an educated organization and the leader. Knowing that they hold much of the information needed to provide solutions to the day-to-day and long-term organizational challenges, others will no longer respond to a dictated approach. Effective leaders know this, too, and take advantage of it. They can change their focus to the strategies and visions to assure success.

*Today I will focus on providing those around me
with the information they need to do their jobs
and helping them develop the skills they
need to make effective decisions.*

DAY
19

*"Coming together is a beginning; keeping together
is progress; working together is success."*

HENRY FORD

*T*eaming has gone from theory to mainstream in most
organizations, yet taking advantage of the synergy of
a group intellect is one of the biggest leadership challenges. People
have different personalities. Motives are often nebulous because
of hidden personal agendas. When conflict arises, many people
have a difficult time confronting the issues.

Teams must be able to talk openly in a safe environment about
any issue that affects their purpose. Hidden agendas, if they exist,
must be exposed. The most effective leaders help their teams by
facilitating communication and confrontation. Indeed, this is the
only way that a group of people can work together.

Leaders must be open to the same level of confrontation and
communication as all others in the team. They must also be open
about their own agendas. True collaboration can only exist when
there is open, true communication within the group.

*I am effective at facilitating communication within the teams
I am involved in. I continually encourage openness as
a primary means to accomplish our purpose.*

DAY 20

---

*"Nobody can be exactly like me. Sometimes
even I have trouble doing it."*
TALLULAH BANKHEAD

*T*here is a strong temptation to surround ourselves
with others who are like us in most ways. It feels safe
and comfortable. If we share the same preferences for auditory,
visual, or kinesthetic communication, we have fewer misunderstandings. When we share many of the same interests, we feel
more secure in our relationship.

Leaders must avoid the urge to do this. We have to take advantage of the multitude of different talents and styles that others
possess. If everyone in our circle is just like us, we will never be
able to see all perspectives of the daily problems and challenges
we face. No matter how talented we are, we cannot do it all; we
have to allow other talented individuals to help us achieve our
vision.

*Today I will focus on the talents and styles of those
around me and find ways to utilize their
specific strengths to complement my own.*

DAY 21

*"You have to do a little bragging on yourself even
to your relatives—man just doesn't get
anywhere without advertising."*
JOHN NANCE GARNER

*W*e are all aware that when we have a great idea, we
have to sell it. In order to gain cooperation on a
new project, we have to promote it. To motivate those we lead,
we give them positive feedback and acknowledge their efforts for
all to see and hear.

Yet when it comes to ourselves, modesty often prevails. We
are taught when growing up that we should never brag.

People do not support ideas alone, however. They do not
cooperate with a project. They support and cooperate with other
people. Leaders must be sure that their credibility is always apparent. We must blow our own horn at times, so that others recognize our talents and accomplishments. Since we do not always
have someone to do that for us, it is important to recognize the
need to do so for ourselves.

*It is important that others recognize my contribution,
and I will find ways to assure that they do.*

DAY 22

---○---

"In general Zeus has so created the nature of the rational animal, that he can attain nothing good for himself, unless he contributes some service to the community."
EPICTETUS

It is easy to become caught up in the day-to-day business of life and not have energy left to devote to our communities. We think that monetary contributions alone will suffice. It is a natural truth that the more you give, the more you receive. When you give of your time and energy to a cause you believe in, to other people, or even to your son's or daughter's sports teams, you will receive incalculable benefits in return. You will also find the energy to do it all.

It is your responsibility as a leader to forge the way. You must demonstrate to those you lead the importance of giving of oneself. Encourage the people you lead to take an active role in their community. It is good for them, and the entire organization benefits from the positive recognition of the stance of giving back.

I will take action today to participate more fully in my community and find ways to encourage those I lead to do the same.

DAY 23

"The rung of a ladder was never meant to rest upon, but only to hold a man's foot long enough to enable him to put the other somewhat higher."
THOMAS HENRY HUXLEY

A leader is responsible for bringing vision to an organization and motivating others to complete it. It is important to remember that vision and goals are not just for the organization. You must be continually on top of your own vision. Staying too long in one place can make you stale and ineffective. In today's environment, leaders must keep moving and developing. There are no guarantees that your position will exist tomorrow.

Where are *you* going? How long will it take *you* to get there? Who is going to help *you*? What skills and abilities do *you* need to develop to reach your personal vision for *yourself*? Questions such as these will help focus or refocus your personal vision. They will keep you moving toward success.

Today I will take action that moves me toward developing a clearer personal vision and doing what I need to do to achieve it.

DAY 24

---

*"Tact is the knack of making a point
without making an enemy."*
HOWARD W. NEWTON

*A*s leaders, we will often be faced with resistance to a certain message or to specific feedback we give someone. Often the resistance is not the result of the message. Instead, the negative reaction may result from the way the message is presented.

As our lives get busier, it becomes easier to forget the impact of our words on others. We try to be more efficient; speed is key. Still, everyone we deal with brings their ego to work, and most egos are very fragile. Being careful to phrase things so that the message gets through while protecting the person receiving the message is one of the most challenging aspects of leadership. We must be easy on the people, yet hard on the issues, and get our message across tactfully.

*I rely on expert communication skills to influence others and
get my message across. I am easy on the people involved,
while still being hard on the issues.*

DAY 25

"I do not know anyone who has got to the top without hard work. That is the recipe. It will not always get you to the top, but it should get you pretty near."
MARGARET THATCHER

*T*he closer and closer you move toward the top, the harder and harder you have to work. Accountability increases with each leap forward. Expectations of performance seem to multiply exponentially. Life gets lonelier. Leaders move forward, however, in spite of the added work and pressure. Being a leader is a calling. Moving ahead is the reward for our talents and efforts.

Remember to continue to push toward your goals. If you become too comfortable with your current situation and surroundings, you may soon be the one being led rather than the one doing the leading. Push a little harder. You have to work smart, but work hard too. It will get you where you want to be.

Today I will focus on ways that I can put in that extra bit of effort that differentiates me and moves me toward my calling.

DAY 26

---

*"Truly there is a tide in the affairs of men; but there
is no gulf-stream setting forever in one direction."*
JAMES RUSSELL LOWELL

*I*t used to be much easier to spot a trend and ride its
wave through to completion. It could be a long ride,
lasting several years or even several decades. Leaders still must be
on the lookout for trends, yet we must be quicker to spot them.
They do not last as long anymore. Our focus has changed from
years and decades to weeks and months.

Much is being said about providing continual improvement
in our products and services. In addition to this trend, leaders
must be willing to come up with something totally new or abandon the old when necessary. You cannot afford to hold on to
what used to work if the direction of the market changes completely. Where are the trends? How should you respond? Be
prepared to concentrate more energy on these questions in the
future.

*I am an expert trend spotter. Today I will take concerted
positive action to respond to trends that affect my
organization and the people I lead.*

DAY 27

When was the last time you really laughed at yourself? So much of our lives is full of irony and slapstick. The pressures of our positions can cloud our perception of the comedy of life. We tend to worry about the impression we leave on others, and seriousness overtakes our actions.

Trying to see the world in a new way opens up our vision and creativity. Look at yourself as an outsider would. Where is there room for a chuckle? What are your idiosyncrasies, and how are they affecting your view of life? Taking yourself and your environment too seriously closes doors and makes life boring. Open up to the funny side, and open up to more creativity.

*Today I will look for the humor and irony in
my actions. I will laugh when I can and not
take everything as seriously as I have.*

DAY 28

---○---

"Don't be afraid to take a big step if one is indicated.
You can't cross a chasm in two small jumps."
DAVID LLOYD GEORGE

*T*here are so many opportunities facing us today. As leaders we need to seize opportunities when they arise. The speed of change can get in the way of our decision-making process. This can be frightening, especially when there is a lot riding on the line. To be sure we are seeing the whole picture, caution is warranted. We have to analyze and evaluate before we decide.

Once you have reached a decision, however, you can seldom afford to be tentative in your action. Competition is often hot on the trail, or the window of opportunity may be small. Take the necessary action. Do it definitively, and do not look back.

There are tremendous opportunities to seize. Today
I will move toward firm, definitive action
in order to take advantage of them.

DAY 29

*"Today's put-off objectives reduce
tomorrow's achievements."*

HARRY F. BANKS

*G*oals and objectives, whether daily or long-term, are
part of the everyday life of all good leaders. In order
to be powerful, you have to associate time frames with your goals.
If you do not set time frames for objectives and goals, you will
greatly diminish the possibility of completing them. When to
complete them will be unclear to you and others, and you will
not take action appropriately.

Far more dangerous are the goals and objectives that have time
frames and action plans yet are not completed by the projected
date. Other things may get in the way, and we postpone completion. Sometimes we do not keep up with them, and they revert
back to being undated.

Keeping up with the time frames associated with objectives is
instrumental to your success. If deadlines cannot be met, which
often happens, then revise the dates. Keep the objectives current.
They move you toward all future achievements.

*Today I will take action to be sure that I am completing my
objectives in a timely manner. They are instrumental to
my success and propel me powerfully into the future.*

DAY 30

---○---

*"It is only in romances that people undergo a sudden
metamorphosis. In real life, even after the most
terrible experiences, the main character
remains exactly the same."*
ISADORA DUNCAN

*M*ost psychologists agree that the major components
of personality are solidified by the time a child is six
years old. This is why we cannot change people. They are who
they are, and they have been that way since childhood.

What we can change is behavior. In order to get people to
respond to changes they need to make, we should make it clear
to them that we value their personality. No matter what the
personality, behaviors that get in the way of optimum performance can be adjusted.

Be specific about the actual behaviors, things that people *say*
or *do*. Let them know what the ineffective behaviors are, but also
describe in detail what the effective behaviors need to be. Then
give people a reason to change. If they do not see a benefit, they
may agree in word but never participate in action.

*I will focus today on providing behaviorally specific feedback and
suggestions to those around me, while showing them that
I value their personality and individual talents.*

DAY
31

"Pessimism leads to weakness; optimism to power."
WILLIAM JAMES

*I*f you read the newspaper or turn on the radio or television, it is astounding how much negativity you will find. More often than not, the news is tragic. Sandwiched between the news and all other programming is an endless litany of advertising that attempts to convince us that we are not happy enough, not sexy enough, not good enough parents or children. This negativity is an attempt to weaken us so that we will buy the particular product being advertised.

It is easy to fall into the trap of negativity. The truth is that you are happy enough, sexy enough, and good enough. Seeing the positive opportunities that surround your every movement and seizing them with hope, optimism, and excitement is much more effective than participating in the negativity that blasts us from all sides. Optimism and positivity move us toward the success we desire.

*Today I will not be victimized by those who stand to gain by
negativity. I will look long and hard at the positive
aspects of the opportunities that come my way.*

DAY 32

"Tell me what you eat and I will tell you what you are."
ANTHELME BRILLAT-SAVARIN

*D*o you have enough energy to accomplish all you would like? Is your concentration on a par with your needs?

Our bodies are like fine machines. The quality of the fuel we provide makes a difference to the way it runs. There are direct parallels to the knocks, pings, and sluggishness that you will see in a car after a tankful of low-octane gasoline and the aches, pains, and lack of energy we feel after consuming low-octane food.

Much is demanded from leaders. You need extra strength and power just to get you through the challenges of each day. Pay attention to what you are putting into your body. It plays a big factor in what you get out of it.

*Beginning today I am even more conscious of the quality
of fuel I provide my body so that it can maintain
the energy and efficiency it needs to carry
out all the responsibilities I force upon it.*

DAY 33

*"It is better to know some of the questions
than all of the answers."*
JAMES THURBER

*I*t is not the job of the leader to know all of the answers.
That is not even possible anymore. Too much information bombards us from all sides. Good leaders learn to ask good questions. Good questions are open-ended and nonjudgmental.

When we ask questions that can be answered with only a yes or a no, we are usually looking for an affirmation of our current belief. If we taint our questions with judgments before we even know the answer, we will find that the answers easily fit our expectations.

Instead, we must openly ask the right questions in a manner that leaves room for good news and bad news. We must listen to the answers and read between the lines. When we think about the questions we need to have answered, we will often find the answers where we least expect them. Formulate the questions openly and then be open to the responses from wherever or whomever they come.

*I realize there is too much information for me to know all the
answers. I am effective at asking the right questions at
the right time, and all the answers are there for me.*

DAY 34

"The secret of a man's being is not only to live
but to have something to live for."
FYODOR DOSTOYEVSKY

What are the underlying principles that guide your life and carry you through your day-to-day existence? How do they affect the choices you make and the direction you take as you contribute to life? Life is an adventure to enjoy, true, but too many people live their lives with no real purpose or meaning. You are in the unique position to inspire others through your actions to live for something greater than themselves.

If you have not already done so, think about your reasons for living. If you have already done so, today would be a great time to evaluate that purpose and see how well you are doing. The need for a purpose is part of our underlying core as humans. Live your purpose and help others see and live theirs.

My purpose is compelling, exciting, and the center of my existence.
By discovering and living my own purpose, I inspire
others to find and live their own.

DAY 35

"You can make more friends in two months by becoming more interested in other people than you can in two years by trying to get people interested in you."
DALE CARNEGIE

*F*riendship is one of the sweetest joys that life offers. You can have all the material success in the world, yet without friends, life will be dull and unfulfilled. Leaders are often high achievers who have gotten to where they are by being driven and competitive. It is easy to transfer this competitive drive into your social life and friendships. Friendships based on competition may work on the tennis court, but in life there must be more.

True caring and mutual desire for the success and happiness of the other define a loving friendship. The mutual celebration of each other's life forms the core. Your interest in other persons, the opposite of competition, is so strong that you want them to win—and they want you to win also.

This level of closeness is hard to achieve but is possible. How many of your friendships are based on caring and mutual support? What can you do to strengthen all your friendships?

There are new ways that I can demonstrate true interest in the lives of my friends. Today I will focus on strengthening my bonds of friendship.

DAY 36

*L*eaders in organizations around the globe are finding
that they are being evaluated and scrutinized as never
before. It is essential for the survival of any organization that the
people affiliated with it constantly update their skills to keep pace
with the rapid changes that are part of every phase of life.

There is no *job* security in the world today, regardless of what
level or skills you've attained. This is true of leaders who work
for an organization, those who own their own, and even those
who volunteer their skills. There is, however, *positional* security.
The way to remain secure in your position is to find ways to
remain at the head of the pack in terms of knowledge.

Learn as much as you can from as many different sources as
you can. Keep pace with the trends. The future is becoming the
present at a faster pace than at any other time in history. No one
can venture into it without learning what is needed to survive.

*Today I will secure my future by urgently finding ways
to discover the new skills that I will need and by
taking action to be sure I learn them.*

DAY 37

*"So live so that you wouldn't be ashamed to sell
the family parrot to the town gossip."*
WILL ROGERS

*P*eople are fascinated with stories about other people. It
is an intrinsic part of human nature. This interest is
healthy when people focus positively on what is happening in
the lives of others out of a true interest to be part of the human
community. Caring about others helps keep the fabric of society
intact. Unfortunately, there is a side of our interest in others that
can be dangerous. People are just as fascinated with the negative
as with the positive.

Leaders must lead impeccable lives. Your lifestyle is under constant scrutiny by those who choose to emulate you as well as by
those who wish to undermine your accomplishments. It is a grave
injustice to lead astray those who would model your behavior. It
can be dangerous to your stability as a leader to give those who
wish to weaken your position the ammunition to do so.

*I make every effort to lead a lifestyle that I am proud
others attempt to imitate and that gives no one
an opportunity to throw stones.*

DAY 38

---○---

*I*n this age of information it is easy to be overcome by data when making decisions. Information overload can slow the decision-making process to a standstill. Several reports on the same issue may be contradictory. Teams will have a difficult time determining the validity of the opportunities they evaluate. Leaders become less sure where to turn for statistics that guarantee a positive outcome. Oddly, it seems that the more information we have, the less clear are our conclusions.

Leaders who do not become paralyzed with the analysis make the best decisions. At some point, these leaders determine they have enough information and go with their gut instinct. Always be aware of what your intuition is telling you. Practice being more sensitive to it. That unexplained feeling from within is frequently right, especially when it is paired with logical facts acquired through investigation and study.

Today I will concentrate on listening to the voice from within when faced with decisions. I will trust my instincts so that they may lead me to the best conclusions.

DAY 39

"Few things help an individual more than to place responsibility upon him and to let him know that you trust him."

BOOKER T. WASHINGTON

No relationship functions when there is a lack of trust. Frequently, we remember times when we have been hurt by someone and transfer those feelings of betrayal to other associates. We do not give them a chance because the last time we gave someone a chance, they took advantage and we were harmed. Although nothing is explicitly stated, people intuitively perceive this absence of confidence. Leaders have so much to do that they must learn to trust, even when it does not come naturally.

Some believe that if you give someone enough rope, they will eventually hang themselves with it. Successful leaders cannot afford to use that paradigm. Instead, give those you lead the rope, and tell them what it is to be used for. Teach them how to tie a few knots. Then have faith that most people will tie tight and secure square knots instead of a noose.

Today I will work to release any fear of trusting the people I rely upon. I will let them know I trust them to successfully fulfill their responsibilities.

DAY 40

"A leader has two important characteristics: first, he is going somewhere; second, he is able to persuade other people to go with him."
ROBESPIERRE

A good leader has a compelling vision that others want to follow. You must constantly be working on your vision and what you are doing to reach it. Vision is like a vacation: Although you know the destination, you still need to decide which routes to take to get there. Once you plan the routing, you need to watch the signs along the way to be sure you are heading in the right direction. Detours to visit an unexpected attraction are fine, but you should revise the routing to be sure you continue along to the final destination after you visit the attraction.

Travel brochures use exhilarating language and vivid photos to attract visitors to exotic destinations. Likewise, you must use rousing language and paint the picture of your vision, too, if you want others to ride along with you on your journey. If you keep your vision compelling enough when you invite others along, they will fly along wherever you want to go.

Today I will examine my vision to be sure that I am still on the right path. I constantly focus on using colorful language and vivid descriptions to motivate others to come along with me.

DAY
41

---○---

"Success isn't a result of spontaneous combustion.
You must set yourself on fire."
ARNOLD GLASOW

*L*eaders have energy and drive that others notice and want to follow. If you take care of yourself and have a cause that is exciting enough, you will find unlimited internal energy resources. You have to self-motivate. Others are not going to be concerned about motivating you. It is your unique position as a leader to access the inward verve and stamina that you have and use it to inspire others.

Take initiative to read about and listen to other successful leaders in order to find your own dynamic enlightenment and strength of purpose. Seek out mentors to guide you and offer direction. Mostly look within. The power is there. Light the flame. Your intense passion will set others into frenzied motion to follow you enthusiastically.

I can access unlimited energy resources within myself.
I will enthusiastically take action today to inspire
others with the flame of my passion.

DAY 42

"Whether you think you can or whether you think you can't, you're right."
HENRY FORD

*H*as anyone ever told you that you could not do something, which made you run right out and do it to prove that they were wrong? Everyone has had that type of experience. It does not matter what others believe. The important consideration is your own belief. Your positive mental image of what is possible will open the path to opportunities that others, because of their own limiting beliefs, would never see.

If it were not for the belief in possibilities in spite of the odds, few of humankind's accomplishments would have been achieved. Few things would happen in any organization if it were not for the adamant belief by someone of the possibilities associated with a new idea. It is your responsibility to challenge your own assumptions at all times. Look for possibilities in the impossible. Believe in the power that we all have to do anything the mind can create.

I will challenge old assumptions today. I profoundly understand the power of my beliefs and find ways to look at new ideas and opportunities in terms of their possibilities.

DAY 43

"Participatory management is harder still on the top manager. Because it is a distinctly empowering style of leadership, the manager must want to share her power."

M. SCOTT PECK

*L*eaders have always been rewarded for being decisive, superior problem solvers and good at inspiring people to follow their lead. The higher up we go, the more "power" comes with the post. This power is intoxicating. Once you have something as exhilarating as power, it is hard to give up.

The changes we are experiencing as we move to an information-based economy have had profound implications on leadership power. Power is now centered in knowledge and in knowing what to do with knowledge. It is no longer possible to hold all the information and be involved in all the decisions. There is too much information. Exceptional leaders know that they must share the power of their positions with those they lead, allowing them to make effective decisions themselves. Leaders must find their reward in helping to develop judgment skills in others rather than making the decisions themselves. The more power you release to others, the more you will be seen as a visionary leader who is able to focus on strategic issues.

I am an empowering leader and give those around me the power they need to be effective.

DAY 44

---

*"Man has no choice but to love. For when he does not,
he finds his alternatives lie in loneliness,
destruction, and despair."*
LEO BUSCAGLIA

*S*eldom is love listed as one of the values that leaders must hold in order to be effective. Maybe this is because it is possible to be effective while ignoring love. We have so many things to do that it is easy to leave out those we love or who love us. We are good leaders because we can handle the emergencies. We are willing to put in the long hours. We "love" what we do.

Do not allow the "love" for what you do to step in the way of your love for other people. The people you love will not always be in your life. They move; they grow; they die. If you ignore them, they will move, grow, and die even quicker. Enjoy them while you can. Love them unconditionally, remembering that their faults are equaled by your own.

Let others into your life, and hold them there. Cherish them, and they will cherish you. Love adds the extra spice, as well as the extra comfort, that makes all you do worthwhile.

*Today I will spend extra energy with those I love. I will
make a call, make a visit, or make a date and let
them know how important they are to me.*

DAY 45

"A journey of a thousand miles begins with a single step."
LAO-TZU

*O*ne of the qualities that separates the best leaders from all the others is their ability to take action when necessary. They learn how to judge when there is enough information. They know that it is possible to talk about ideas forever, but talk is cheap, and nothing gets done by just talking about it. The best leaders have goals, and they move on them.

What ideas or projects are you putting off because you do not feel you have enough information? Are you talking about projects but not taking action because of fear, uncertainty, or doubt? Do your goals seem so far away that you dare not move because it may take too much energy to get where you want to be?

You must make the first step. That first step will start the momentum going. It may be difficult, but once you are rolling along toward that goal, idea, or project, it will seem silly that you waited so long to make the first move.

Today is my day for action. I will take a first step toward an important goal, idea, or action.

DAY 46

---○---

*T*here is no doubt that leaders must possess excellent persuasion skills. Essential to persuasion is our ability to be superior communicators. Constantly work on your ability to communicate to others. Take classes. Join Toastmasters. Ask others for feedback.

When you find that someone did not understand what you told them, do not blame them for not listening. Blame yourself for not presenting a motivating message that inspires them to listen.

Whether you are talking to one person or one thousand, your words carry the message. Make them powerful. Make them eloquent. Be responsible with them, and be sure that they convey who you are and what you represent.

*Today I will concentrate on what I can do to be
a better communicator so that I inspire
others with my ideas and my passion.*

DAY
47

*"A hundred times every day I remind myself that my
inner and outer life are based on the labors of other
men, living and dead, and that I must exert
myself in order to give in the same measure
as I have received and am still receiving."*
ALBERT EINSTEIN

*T*hink of all the people who have made it possible for
you to be where you are at this moment. Trying to
add them up is mind boggling. There were teachers who opened
your mind, ministers or rabbis who opened your spirit, mentors
who opened doors, friends who opened your heart, and others
who opened the way. They may have briefly been in your life.
They may have been there all the time. They all shared a common
interest—that you excel and prosper as a person.

Sometimes it may feel as though you are all alone. For every
leader, however, there has been a vast network of others who
have made the climb possible. They supported, encouraged,
pushed, and let go. Remember them. Without them, the path
to leadership would have been even rockier and steeper. Let them
know how important they have been to you and that you appreciate them. You are here because they were and are there.

*Today, in thought or deed, I will make it a point to show my
appreciation to someone who has made a difference
in my life and who deserves my gratitude.*

DAY 48

*"Integrity is keeping the small promises
we make to ourselves."*
RICHARD LEIDER

So much is made of the word *integrity.* It is often confused with the word *honesty.* Actually, they are different words. *Honesty* is keeping promises we make to others. *Integrity* is keeping the promises we make to ourselves.

It is a challenge to live our lives with true integrity. It is easy to find justifications to veer off from our values when it seems convenient. We are often weakest when we think others are not looking or are not aware of our actions.

By not keeping promises we make to ourselves, we lose self-respect, just as we would lose the respect of others by not keeping promises we make to them. Live with true integrity. Fight the tendency to justify actions that are incongruent with your values. You may think that no one but you will know, but our souls are as transparent as the air we breathe. The confidence and self-respect you exude as a result of being true to yourself will be evident to all around you and will draw a trust that words and deeds alone could never accomplish.

*I am a person with true integrity. Today I will be sure
to take action on the promises I make to myself.*

DAY 49

*"Never doubt that a small group of thoughtful,
committed citizens can change the
world. Indeed, it is the only
thing that ever has."*

MARGARET MEAD

Whether you are part of a team, committee, or informal group, chances are you are leading change somewhere. Resistance to change can be discouraging. The means are so difficult, and the end seems so far away.

As long as the change is justified, those who resist it are weakened by the mere presence of their resistance. They are the ones who do not at this moment have the courage to face the inevitable. They assume that fighting change is less painful than the change itself. However, the energy it takes to carry on a battle for an unjust cause is far greater than the energy it takes to bring about just change that is for the greater good.

Keep up your struggle. You may feel outnumbered, but your cause carries more power than all the force of their resistance. Be patient. The shore may seem far away, but the tide is coming in and you are the one riding the wave headed straight for the shore.

*I have all the strength I need to carry through the positive
changes that I am leading. Others follow my lead
because of the justness of my cause.*

DAY 50

"Most people don't plan to fail; they fail to plan."
JOHN L. BECKLEY

*I*t is crucial to have goals and purpose. As a leader, you must have a compelling vision that motivates others to follow. Without a plan that is precise and realistic, however, you will not accomplish these things.

A plan is like a road map. It lets you know how you are getting to where you want to go. You refer to it periodically to be sure you are still on the right road and to know when you leave one road to get on another. The map also lets you take advantage of the various routings that may get you to the same place.

You must not plan only one obvious route. Plan also for possible roadblocks and alternate routes that can take you where you are going.

It helps if others have a copy of the plan and can participate in selecting the route, especially if they are along for the ride. On any trip, not having a road map is the surest way to become confused and distracted at every fork in the road.

I continually review my plans to be sure they take into account all the options and obstacles I may face along the way.

DAY 51

"Life is not so short but that there is time for courtesy."
RALPH WALDO EMERSON

*M*any people touch our lives in a special way. They make it easier for us to be leaders. A hotel receptionist may upgrade your room just because you look tired after a long trip. Your assistant may field that important call in an exceptional way that saves a crucial piece of business. An associate may put you in touch with a key person who will assist you in growing even further in your role as a leader. Your spouse, friend, or child may give you a back rub just when you need it.

When the occasion warrants, there is nothing so appreciated as a warm thank you. The people in your life who do any special thing for you deserve it. Send thank-you notes whenever you can. Do it as soon as possible after you receive the favor. Not only is it a courtesy, but it is also good business. Long after the person forgets what the good deed was, he or she will remember getting a thank-you note from you.

I am appreciative of what others do for me, and I make
sure I show my appreciation promptly. Today I
will send some overdue thank-you notes.

DAY 52

"No one can become really educated without having pursued some study in which he took no interest—for it is a part of education to learn to interest ourselves in subjects for which we have no aptitude."

T. S. ELIOT

*O*ne of the reasons why you are in your position is because of your unique talents. Naturally, you are motivated to make the most of those talents. You are good at them. You like doing them. They come easily to you. Generally you are recognized and rewarded for having those talents.

If you rely solely on your areas of natural expertise, you will not be completely effective. All leaders must develop in new areas that may be difficult for them. If you do not have a natural aptitude, you may find that you do not have any interest in growing in some critical areas. You may feel that you are unable to. There may be some fear of failure. Identify the crucial skills that are outside your talent base. Force yourself to spend time to master them. You must be well rounded in order to make the exceptional judgments that are expected of you.

I am capable of learning any new skill I am willing to work hard enough on. I will take action today to develop in crucial areas where I am not completely comfortable.

DAY 53

"The ultimate point of creative visualization is to make every moment of our lives a moment of wondrous creation, in which we are just naturally choosing the best, the most beautiful, the most fulfilling lives we can imagine."
SHAKTI GAWAIN

Nothing happens without it first being visualized. An idea moves from a concept in someone's head, through to action, and on to completion. The brain cannot tell the difference between the real and the imagined, and our subconscious mind will do everything in its power to narrow the gap. What we choose to see as our future is unmistakably what we create.

What is it that you want for yourself and for your world? Create it in your own mind. See it clearly. Concentrate on your future and see it in brilliant colors. The brighter you can envision your desires, the more likely it is that you will attract and recognize opportunities to bring your own imagined reality to a physical reality.

Everyone visualizes. Some take control of it and some do not. Take control. See the positive and the best. Bring the future to you by imagining it first in all its possibilities. Then act to make sure you are always moving toward it.

Today I concentrate on envisioning the future clearly and brightly in my mind.

DAY 54

"Life is either a daring adventure or nothing. Security does not exist in nature, nor do the children of men as a whole experience it. Avoiding danger is no safer in the long run than exposure."

HELEN KELLER

*T*oo many people spend their lives trying to avoid risk. They make safe decisions. They look for guarantees in everything they do. There are no guarantees in life, though, and the higher the risk, the higher the potential payback. But you have to be an optimist to take advantage of that philosophy.

Sometimes we run from risk because of a fear of losing something. The irony is nothing is stable anyway, and we can lose whatever it is we fear losing just by doing nothing. The big gains in life come with a sense of adventure and daring, a fearlessness.

Go for the gain. Overcome your fears of loss. Think it through. Calculate the risk, then take it. The payback could be great. You will never know until you try.

I am excited about the gains I could obtain by being more adventurous and taking more risks. Today I will take a risk that I may not have taken before.

DAY 55

---○---

"Something unknown is doing we know not what."
SIR ARTHUR EDDINGTON

We are not in control of everything. Even with all the planning in the world, it is impossible to predict the gifts we receive to help us along the way or the obstacles that mysteriously present themselves just when we thought everything was going perfectly.

If you examine the evidence in your personal history, you will find that everything happens for a reason. We can learn from all adversity. We can also learn to tune in to the gifts and nudges that come our way to help us in our efforts. Be aware of them. Realize that there is a force that is working behind the scenes, paving the way when we are ready to have the way paved. Do not rush it, but recognize it when it comes. Call on it when you need it. Take advantage of it. It is a special, powerful force for you.

Today I will acknowledge the mysterious force in my life that gives me the added hand when I need it. I am aware and thankful for its presence.

DAY 56

When things do not turn out as expected, it is natural to look for the underlying reason why. This works fine when we look at ourselves, but many direct blame exclusively outside of themselves. We have all heard of people involved in spouse or child abuse, claiming that the reason why they do it is because their parents abused them. Blaming one's parents rather than taking personal responsibility for ending the cycle is twisted reasoning.

This flawed logic of blame sometimes occurs in our positions as leaders. Things are bound to go wrong. People make mistakes, and it is easy to find someone to blame for mistakes. But there is no need for blame; there is only a need for learning from mistakes. Instead of using negative energy to look for fault, convert the energy to something positive. Look for things to praise in people. Reward them for their successes. Keep your focus positive and praise freely, and those around you will work harder, longer, and with fewer mistakes. They will be more secure and give you more reasons to praise. It is a powerful and successful tool.

*I am known for praising others when things go well
rather than placing blame when they do not.*

DAY 57

---○---

"Genius, that power which dazzles mortal eyes,
Is oft but perseverance in disguise."
HENRY AUSTIN

*A*s a culture we are attracted to the brightness of intelligence. To be around someone who can analyze a problem and find solutions with speed and clarity exhilarates us. Rarely are solutions and problems easy to identify immediately. And identifying them is only half the battle because solutions are rarely simple or easy. People like Thomas Edison and Albert Einstein spent years doggedly testing theories and ideas. Their greatness was due in part to their willingness to keep going on when most others would have thrown in the towel.

Real genius lies in the ability to stick with ideas and visions tenaciously. It is one thing to identify easy solutions to problems and quite another to do what is necessary to test the solutions, evaluate their effectiveness, and carry them through to the end.

At times I may be tempted to give up, but I will not.
The test of my genius rests in my determination
to persevere and overcome all obstacles.

DAY 58

---○---

"There is nothing either good or bad,
but thinking makes it so."
WILLIAM SHAKESPEARE,
HAMLET, ACT 2, SCENE 2

*S*uccessful people have the ability to find the good in anything. In a world full of change, worry, and tragedies, good leaders help others to find the value in all situations. We are bombarded daily with pessimistic news reports of local and world events. Our organizations may be going through change that is changing people's lives in ways that may cause them pain. These circumstances make it more important than ever for leaders to point to the good.

It is the responsibility of leaders to help others, who may have difficulties doing so for themselves, see the worth of any situation. First you must believe yourself that there is positive value. Otherwise, you will be as transparent as glass, and your facade will be as easy to break. Both the positive and the negative are there if you look for them. Find and communicate the value of what may appear to others as negative. Your ability to do so is necessary for their mental health.

I see the positive aspects of any situation, and I am able to
communicate them to people who may not see for themselves.

DAY 59

"The speed of the leader is the speed of the gang."
MARY KAY ASH

*L*ately our world seems like a ride in a race car with no brakes. The outside world is a blur as we speed by. The turns are treacherous, and it takes an enormous amount of concentration just to stay on the track. While at times it may be a frightening ride, there is no turning back.

Everything we deal with demands more attention in shorter amounts of time. We can blame it on technology or unrealistic expectations, but the cause does not matter. Our world seems to move even faster every day, and it is not going to change.

We must help others speed through the processes that are necessary to keep on the track. They will follow our lead. They may not always like it, but they will stay on the path we blaze. Circumstances demand that we be on this path. We cannot go back. In order to survive, the leader must maintain a velocity that keeps pace with the competition while teaching others how to keep their eyes on the road, steer around the corners, and maneuver through tight spots. You set the pace. Help your team keep up with the rest of the world and win the race.

I am responsible for helping my team keep up with the fast pace in the world. My actions help to keep us on the leading edge and ahead of the competition.

DAY 60

"The man who does not read good books has no advantage over the man who can't read them."

MARK TWAIN

You have to be on top of the trends, or you will lead others down paths that are long overgrown and abandoned. One of the most effective ways to stay up on trends is by reading. Newspapers keep you up on daily current events and give you an indication of what is on your customers' minds. Magazines and trade journals consolidate useful information on the implications of current events both in and around your field of expertise. Books detail everything. They all predict and influence the course of events that shape our lives.

This all sounds so simple, until your reading pile gets so thick it seems that you will never get through it. So you ignore it, toss it, or save it in a heap waiting for the day you can dedicate to nothing other than reading. Of course that day seldom, if ever, comes. Try a little at a time. Dedicate a specific time each day to keep up with your reading. It will keep you fresh. You will be more alert. You will make better decisions. You will be better informed as to where to lead those who are depending on your skills and knowledge.

Today I will read something that will help me as a leader. I keep up on my reading, for it is the way for me to keep up with the trends that shape my world.

DAY
61

---○---

"If one is lucky, a solitary fantasy can totally transform one million realities."
MAYA ANGELOU

When we were children, our lives were full of fantasies. They consumed our lives. They made everything imaginable possible. Our youthful fantasies were encouraged, and, we thought, someday they would be reality.

Somewhere along the line, reality began overpowering our fancy. Maybe our imaginations were overcome with the physical evidence that contradicted our fantasies. Perhaps we were told to grow up and give up the imaginary worlds that entertained us. For some of us, giving up our fantasies meant that we also stopped imagining the possibilities in the unseen and unproven world. We grew up!

Fantasies can come true. Our imaginations can create a world that no one else can see. It only takes acting on the dream of one person to change the world. If you have a dream or a fantasy, do not give it up for logic. Make it happen. Overcome reality and make the world a better place.

Today I reconnect with my dreams. I will find ways to make my fantasies overcome current realities and make life better for others and myself.

DAY 62

---○---

*"Associate with men of good quality, if you esteem
your own reputation, for it is better to be
alone than in bad company."*
GEORGE WASHINGTON

One of the biggest challenges a leader faces is assessing other people. Be careful who you choose to allow into your circle. As you continue to grow as a leader, you will be judged by the alliances you have with others. Be strategic in selecting who will be part of that union. Their strengths will become your strengths purely by the power of association. Conversely, their weaknesses will also become aligned with you.

The more powerful you become, the more people will attempt to get into your circle. Choose your associates carefully and strategically. Consider their integrity the ultimate test. Your reputation rides in tandem with theirs.

*I surround myself with people of integrity and
with like values. My strength as a leader
is reflected by those I allow in my circle.*

DAY 63

We live in an abundant world. Time and again people have demonstrated that whatever it is that the mind can believe, the flesh can achieve. Are you becoming all you are capable of being? Sometimes it seems like it takes too much energy to accomplish everything that our heart desires, so we compromise our ambition for ease.

You can have anything. It does not necessarily take more effort than you are already exerting. What it takes is a belief that you can create any reality for yourself that you want. It takes an unwillingness to settle for anything less than you feel you deserve. It takes a drive that overcomes physical and mental obstacles.

The world is yours. Conquer it. Do not let your dreams fade because you concede to less. Make it all happen. Ride your ambition to the stars!

*I believe in a world of abundance, and I am capable of great
things. Today I will be conscious that my ambition is
high enough to achieve all that I can be.*

DAY
64

---

*"Life is like a game of poker: If you don't put any
in the pot, there won't be any to take out."*
MOMS MABLEY

*L*eaders make many heavy investments. In this age of
immediate gratification it is hard to be patient and wait
for them to pay off. What investments? There is the investment
of time. You may be able to get a hamburger in twenty seconds,
but a reputation takes a long time to develop and demonstrate.
There is the investment in learning. Nothing great happens without
out the skills to manage the greatness. There is the investment
in people. They help you get where you want to go.

Any investment is a gamble. The higher the potential earnings,
the higher the risk. As in any investment, the more you study
the market, the players, and the potential, the more you minimize the risk associated with it. Make the investment. Be patient
for the payback. Gamble for the highest gain, but be careful.
Continually analyze the game as you play.

*Today I will think about the investments I am making in time,
learning, and people. I will increase my investments where
I need to so I can assure the highest possible payback.*

DAY 65

"To jaw-jaw is better than to war-war."
WINSTON CHURCHILL

We all have people in our lives whom we disagree with to the point of carrying on a personal war. The struggle goes on continually and saps our strength and resources. Usually the combat is covert. Although we are aware of the conflict, confrontation is indirect, and the battle is carried on behind the scenes.

A tremendous amount of energy is wasted by conflict that is not brought through to full confrontation. In the struggles you face, make the implicit explicit. Talk with the offending (or offended) party. Negotiate regarding the issues you disagree about. Little gets done when two parties are spending their assets, both physical and mental, on hostility. Make up with your foes. Come to terms so that your energies can be focused in a positive manner.

Today I will take action to confront any conflict I am involved in. By pledging to end any personal wars I will have more strength and resources to dedicate to my vision and goals.

DAY 66

---○---

"Growth's fine, but watch out: A cat that chokes to death on cream is just as dead as any other cat."
JOHN P. GRIER

*T*here are natural inhibitors to growth, whether organizational or personal. Money, resources, market factors, and politics all affect the inherent rate of expansion. Our own ability to manage the people and situations involved can restrict the speed at which we develop. Effective leaders are careful to not lose control of growth.

Growth, like a plant, has an innate momentum that must be respected. Too much fertilizer on a vegetable plant will cause it to bloom profusely. Yet the structure cannot support the added potential, and when the blooms fall, no vegetable will appear. The bud just withers. Eventually the plant outgrows itself and dies after a fruitless existence.

Be aware of the natural rhythms of your own growth. Let it happen at its own maximum pace. The fruit it bears will exceed the result of any forced growth.

Growth is a desirable outcome of effective leadership as long as the pace is managed. I am aware of the natural rate and do not force growth against its inherent nature.

DAY 67

"A man may safely venture on his way, who
is so guided that he cannot stray."

SIR WALTER SCOTT

*E*mpowerment is a key concept for the modern leader. To many it means that leaders should unilaterally relinquish responsibilities to others. This is abdication, not empowerment, and it is a dangerous thing to do.

You do need to empower others so that you can focus on complicated issues and strategies. It is also your responsibility to be sure that they have the necessary skills and tools to carry on the tasks you empower them to perform.

If you expect others to be accountable, teach them well so that they are not destined to fail through no fault of their own. Give guidelines. Make sure they know the path well before sending them to forge their way alone. You rely on them to succeed. They need your help to thrive in empowerment so that you can concentrate on the big picture.

I make sure that those I lead have the tools and
skills they need to be empowered so that I
can concentrate on strategic issues.

DAY 68

---

*"I have had a long, long life full of troubles, but there
is one curious fact about them—nine-tenths
of them never happened."*
ANDREW CARNEGIE

*I*t is amazing how much your attitude affects the out-
comes of life. Every obstacle that crosses your path can
be considered either good or bad. No one can argue that life is
full of barriers and restrictions. Without them, though, there
would be little challenge or excitement in anything we do.

It all boils down to how you choose to perceive your world.
If you see the cup as half empty, it will be as you see it. If you
see it as half full, you will be able to envision the eventual filling
of the cup to overflowing. You will be right regardless of the
viewpoint you choose. Still, growth and development only come
through seeing the possibilities. It makes sense to elect to notice
the opportunities manifest in the challenges life presents.

*I see opportunities where others might see problems and learn from
obstacles that block my way. In this way troubles are minimized
for me and I motivate others with my positive outlook.*

DAY 69

"Anyone who takes himself too seriously always runs the risk of looking ridiculous; anyone who can consistently laugh at himself does not."
VACLAV HAVEL

*L*ife is too short to be taken seriously. Even if it were not short it makes sense that the more we learn to laugh at the ironies and circumstances of our lives, the more fun it will be to live.

The great playwrights, authors, and poets have always known this. Many of the greatest comedies ever written were based on tragic circumstances. Laughing at the stresses of life relieves the tension. When you are too serious you draw attention to yourself in a prudish way that others clearly see. They will find ways to relieve the tension if you do not, and you may be the butt of the tittering. Even if this is not the case, unrelieved stress and tension turn into ulcers and headaches. Laugh. Enjoy. Relax and see the humor all around you.

Today I will be sure to look for the humor in everyday events. I am able to laugh in wonderment at the ironies of life and encourage the laughter of others whom I influence.

DAY 70

"The trick in life is to decide what's your major aim—to be rich, a golf champion, world's best father, etc. Once that's settled, you can get on with the happy, orderly process of achieving it."
STANLEY GOLDSTEIN

*G*ood leaders have a vision not only for their organization but also for themselves. They find their passion and work adamantly toward attaining it. It is important to periodically review your passion. As life progresses it is only natural for priorities to change.

Any desire can be achieved. It takes a plan. When your goals and passions change or are redefined, you also have to change the strategy you have to get you there. What is your passion? When was the last time you reviewed your life honestly and checked your priorities?

There is no time like now. Happiness comes while we are on the path to success—not when we are there. Knowing your passion and having a plan keeps you on that path.

Today I will find time to think about my passion and review my priorities. I find contentment in the achievement of the plans I set to fulfill my own personal bliss.

DAY 71

---

*"I saw the angel in the marble and
I chiseled until I set it free."*
MICHELANGELO BUONARROTI

*L*eadership duties are like artistic endeavors. We work
with raw materials to create a masterpiece. Our most
important raw material is people. They are the essence of whatever
leaders attempt to build. You cannot accomplish all of your goals
alone. Their talents, energy, and abilities are what allow you to
advance. They help you make everything happen.

What are you seeing in the people you rely on? What is under-
neath the rough stone facade you see daily? Is there an angel
waiting to be released?

Set free the angel that resides in those you work with. Help
them find their inner strengths and talents. Work with them
as they develop and grow. Set their spirits soaring toward your
compelling vision, and they will help you create a masterwork
like none other.

*I am able to see the hidden talents and abilities in
those I work with. I continually take action
to help them grow and develop.*

DAY 72

"He who is afraid of a thing gives it power over him."
MOORISH PROVERB

What fears are you harboring that are getting in the way of your ultimate great accomplishments? We all have fears. They protect us when we are in danger. They keep us alert in times of trouble. However important it is to have a certain amount of fear, we usually have too much.

Most fears are unjustified. Rather than using them to protect our physical well-being, we use them as a defense mechanism for our psyche. Fear of rejection, fear of failure, fear of success, fear of mental anguish, and all the other psychological fears serve only to prevent us from taking action.

Psychological fears take power over our lives. They control us to the extent that we become ineffective and unable to reach our full potential. Do a fear check. What is causing inaction on your part? Release the fear. It will not help you get where you want to go. It will block every step you take for no reason other than the presence of the fear itself.

Today I will examine areas where I am delaying action to see what fears are blocking my movement. I release those fears so that they no longer have power over me.

DAY 73

"One lie will destroy a whole reputation for integrity."
BALTASAR GRACIÁN

Occasionally we tell small lies in the belief that we are protecting ourselves, others, or our organization. It is easy to justify a lie when you perceive that the truth may be damaging and that fabrication offers protection. This does not work. Most lies are discovered, leading to even worse consequences than the truth would have caused.

When you deceive others and they find out about it, they will never fully trust you again. They may <u>forgive</u>, especially if you are good at justifying the reasoning behind the duplicity. They will never <u>forget</u>, however. Solely because you tried to protect someone or something, your character could be permanently defamed. Truth is the only justifiable way of protecting people. It protects them while protecting you at the same time.

I seek only truthfulness when dealing with others, even about sensitive issues. Truth is the legitimate protector of my character and reputation.

DAY 74

"What is more mortifying than to feel that you have missed the plum for want of courage to shake the tree?"
LOGAN PEARSALL SMITH

*C*ourage is one of the great virtues of leaders. It takes a lot of guts to face the hard issues and take the firm stands. Without courage you will be weak in all you attempt to do. With courage you can accomplish anything. You can leap effortlessly over any obstacle that gets in your way. You can inspire others to follow because of your unbelievable strength of conviction.

Are you doing all that you can to be courageous? Do your associates see you as courageous? Are you willing to fight for what is right? You should energize others with your willingness to take on tough issues. Courageous people step out of the safety zone. They put themselves at risk when justice is at stake. Analyzing the risks and avoiding unnecessary gambling, they do not hesitate to take action when prudent and necessary.

I thrive as a leader because I am known for my courageous demeanor and my willingness to take risks when necessary for the good of my people and my organization.

DAY 75

"I use not only all the brains I have but all I can borrow."

WOODROW WILSON

*O*ne of the biggest challenges most leaders face is the temptation to do everything themselves. Leaders often attempt to perform all tasks because they are confident of their own abilities and feel they are in control when they take on as many tasks as possible. Actually, they have less control. Doing it all, they are not aware of all the variables. They cannot effectively manage their time. Problems and opportunities fall through the cracks because no one is watching for them.

Maximize the ways you can work in partnership with others to reach your goals and visions. Reach out to people who have the skills and talents that dovetail with your own. You will have more control operating in a synergistic fashion than you ever will trying to keep your finger on every pulse. Take advantage of the available brain trust. You will accomplish a vast amount more than what one mere mortal can.

The brain trust available to me is one of my most valuable assets. Today I will find new ways to partner with others who have the skills and talents I need to accomplish my vision.

PETER MENDICH — GENE ATKINSON

DAY 76

---○---

*"The irrationality of a thing is no argument against
its existence, rather a condition of it."*
FRIEDRICH NIETZSCHE

Much of the world makes no sense when we view it from our perspective. We usually cannot get a broad enough view of situations to truly analyze the implications of every aspect of it. There are too many variables. Too many changes. Actually, much of the world we face is pretty chaotic.

When you accept chaos as the norm, it becomes easier to make order out of it. The order comes from developing an ability to categorize and plan not just for the expected but also for the unexpected. Try to get a broader picture of the whole system, not just your small part of it. Anything can happen at any time, with no apparent reason. Your job is to be prepared, and have those on your team prepared, with plans to deal with the unforeseen in as logical a way as possible.

Out of the order we attempt to create, chaos looms naturally. I am able to handle ambiguity and irrationality by accepting the limits of my perceptions and planning for the unexpected.

DAY 77

"What is so certain of victory as patience?"
SELMA LAGERLÖF

*O*ur world demands quicker responses than ever. Customers yell for faster service and speedier replies. Sometimes, no matter what our demands are, we cannot hurry the pace any more than is naturally possible. Yet, because of the pressures from above, below, and around us, we feel an immense urgency to speed up everything even more.

How do you compromise between the need for breakneck solutions for every situation and the natural progression of resolution that cannot be hurried by anyone? Begin by prioritizing what really needs to be done so speedily. Accept the governing laws of the rhythm of nature. Do what you can do. That is all you can do. Acceptance is the means, combined with a little diplomacy with the others whose impatience you must deal with.

I accept that there are some things that cannot be forced. I am able to convey a cool and calm patience to others so that their hastiness does not obstruct the quality of the result.

DAY 78

"To believe in something not yet proved and to underwrite it with our lives; it is the only way we can leave the future open."
LILLIAN SMITH

*F*ew new technologies or inventions were the result of extensive market surveys to determine a demand and earnings potential. If we relied on consumers to tell us what their needs were, we would not have progressed very far. Did consumers know they needed microwave ovens before they existed? What about portable radios and cassette players? Could they have told a market researcher that they needed the automobile or that they needed to be able to fly through the air between continents in a matter of hours? Did they know they needed soup in a can?

If you have an idea, and believe in it with all your heart, that may be all the proving you need. Sometimes our need to verify every new concept or idea with extensive analysis only serves to get in the way of innovation by providing conflicting, confusing, or inaccurate data. Your ideas can change the future. Take control, believe in them, and act on them. Shape the world.

I will not discount my ideas and beliefs solely because of extensive analysis. Analysis is a useful tool, but my heart is the ultimate judge.

DAY 79

―――――○―――――

*"The man who makes no mistakes does
not usually make anything."*
BISHOP W. C. MAGEE

*H*ow comfortable are you with allowing others to make mistakes? Do you punish or celebrate mistakes? No one learns by doing things right. Learning occurs when you allow people to make mistakes. Effective and empowering leaders permit others to make mistakes and to accept the consequences of them as part of the cost of doing business.

If the people on your team fear your reaction when they make mistakes, the ensuing results from their mistakes will be horrible. Fearful people cover up blunders, causing them to be repeated or exacerbated because no one learns from them. Celebrate mistakes as a way to develop people. Make them feel comfortable being honest about their errors. Your losses in the long run will be much smaller, and the skills gained will be much greater.

*I celebrate mistakes as long as we continually learn
from them so we do not repeat them. As a leader
I excel in my responsibility to facilitate
the resulting learning process.*

DAY 80

---○---

"It often happens that I wake at night and begin to think about a serious problem and decide I must tell the Pope about it. Then I wake up completely and remember that I am the Pope."
POPE JOHN XXIII

*T*he buck stops with the leader. It can be lonely to be the one at the top of the totem pole. Leadership roles often develop so quickly in our own minds that it seems unbelievable to ourselves that we have arrived where we are. The challenges are vast. The problems sometimes seem never ending. The final decisions often rest with you.

Never lose sight of the importance of your position. You are special to have gotten to this point in your life. Rejoice in the opportunity you have to do the extraordinary. When the loneliness is too much, or the impact of your position too great, take comfort in the good you are able to accomplish. You are doing what you do because of your unique talent to lead others with passion, compassion, and intelligence.

I am uniquely able to handle the pressures associated with leadership and am respected for my abilities to accomplish great things.

DAY
81

———○———

*"Your own resolution to success is more important
than any other one thing."*
ABRAHAM LINCOLN

Your own personal vision carries the day. No matter
what anyone says. No matter what the newspapers
print. No matter what the analysts predict. You are the deciding
factor in interpreting your dreams and what to do about them.

People are in need of leaders with exciting visions. They will
go the extra mile for a leader committed to succeed regardless of
the odds or obstacles. They will ignore all outside factors if your
determination is strong enough and clear enough. Forget what
the naysayers are talking about. You, more than any other factor,
are responsible for the success you deserve and can so clearly see.

*I am committed to success and the completion of my strong and
clear vision. My determination serves to continually
motivate others as well as myself.*

DAY 82

*"The world is moving so fast these days that the
man who says it can't be done is generally
interrupted by someone doing it."*
HARRY EMERSON FOSDICK

*A*s recently as a decade ago, few could have imagined
the world as we know it today. The changes in overall
lifestyle are astounding and generally a testament to the adaptability of the human race. We keep up with it and have even adapted
to accept and expect change to continue at an even faster pace.

Those who have brought us those changes were mavericks.
They saw the train of change coming and leapt aboard to develop
new products, services, and infrastructures. Unfortunately, many
people refuse to accept the inevitability of change. Rather than
jump aboard the train, they stand on the tracks trying to stop it,
getting run over instead. Jump aboard the train. It will be a fast,
hair-raising experience. You cannot stop it, so you might as well
enjoy the ride.

*Today I will examine my actions to determine where I am resisting
change. Through my adaptability, I am able to be an
example to others who may resist the inevitable.*

DAY 83

―――○―――

"Drive thy business or it will drive thee."
BENJAMIN FRANKLIN

Nobody likes to be manipulated by other people. They will resist any effort by others to take away their free will. Families break up when someone is too controlling. Wars have been fought to protect nations from the domination of outside forces.

When it comes to business or careers, though, many are willing to ride the stream wherever it takes them. Often they are just busy and one day turns into another. Then days become weeks, and weeks become months. Years can go by before they realize that nature itself will manipulate their business in the same manner that they would never allow another human to manipulate their personal life.

Be sure that you take control of your business and career. Otherwise you may wake up one day to discover that it took on a life of its own, and it is a life you never would have chosen.

Today I will take action to update my business and career plans.
I continually take care to monitor my plans and to be
in control of where I am going.

DAY 84

"I had six honest serving men
They taught me all I knew:
Their names were Where and What and When
and Why and How and Who."
RUDYARD KIPLING

*T*he quality of the decisions you are able to make is dependent on the quality of the information you have to analyze. You only get quality answers if you are willing to ask quality questions. Open, in-depth questions examining the causes of problems and the risks and benefits of opportunities must be continually asked. Leaders ask the right kinds of questions and are willing to hear the answers.

Downfalls occur when leaders stop asking questions and start doing all the telling. They falter when they make it difficult for others to give honest answers for fear of looking like they are not on the band wagon or for fear of retribution if they do not give the desired answer.

How skilled are you at asking quality, probing questions? How comfortable have you made others feel about answering, even if the information is painful or unwelcome? Work on being sure those around you know you want truthful answers to even the toughest questions.

Today I will consciously improve the quality of questions I ask
of myself and others. I make others comfortable
to be honest with me at all times.

DAY 85

---

*"I used to work at the International House of Pancakes.
It was a dream and I made it happen."*
PAULA POUNDSTONE

*I*t is simple to make your dreams come true. You just have to identify them and work toward them. What you have to remember in the process is to be careful of what you dream about, because it will come true. Be sure that you are aiming high enough. Be sure you will want to be where your dream takes you.

Remember, too, that you can always change directions. Once you have accomplished your dream, it is time to evaluate things. Decide if you are happy with the outcome. Decide whether you want to continue on the same path or follow another completely different path. The world is yours to have. Make it what you want it to be.

*I am confident in my ability to reach any outcome I can dream.
By achieving my dreams I am able to create greater
opportunities than many think possible.*

DAY 86

---○---

"Injustice, poverty, slavery, ignorance—these may be cured by reform or revolution. But men do not live only by fighting evils. They live by positive goals, individual and collective, a vast variety of them, seldom predictable, at times incompatible."
SIR ISAIAH BERLIN

*P*eople often focus on only what is wrong with the world. Granted, there is injustice wherever one turns. You only need to open a newspaper, turn on a television, or walk down a city sidewalk to see so for yourself. It is easy to focus on the negative and become caught up in the magnitude of problems in the world.

Being aware of the ills of society can make you feel powerless in the wake of it all. Instead, concentrate on what you would like to see changed. Center your energies on the things you can do to make a contribution. You alone may not cure homelessness, hunger, war, or abuse, but you can make an impact. The tide will turn when enough caring people strive to make positive change.

I am a caring and giving person. Today I will take action, no matter how insignificant my effort seems now, toward making the world a better place.

DAY 87

"Take calculated risks. That is quite different from being rash."

GEORGE S. PATTON

*R*isk taking is an essential value of a leader. A leader has to be courageous. If you are going to ask others to follow, you have to be willing to take the first jump yourself into the unknown. But taking risks is not synonymous with being irrational.

Never jump off a cliff without reasonable assurance of survival. Look over the edge to try to determine how far it is to the bottom. Use a parachute or glider to make the jump smooth and increase chances of survival. Choose, perhaps, to walk carefully down the face of the cliff, clutching overgrowth along the way. If you are going to jump off a cliff, be sure to plan a safe way to the bottom. At least be relatively sure that there is something soft to land on after the jump.

I am willing to take the risks that are necessary to go boldly into the future. I am careful, however, not to unnecessarily endanger myself or others in the process.

DAY 88

*"I find the great thing in this world is not so much
where we stand, as in what direction we are
moving: To reach the port of heaven,
we must sail sometimes with the
wind and sometimes against it—
but we must sail, and not
drift, nor lie at anchor."*
OLIVER WENDELL HOLMES

The winds of change are constantly blowing from all directions. You start a project one day, and a week later you have to abandon the whole thing for one reason or another. When this happens too often, it is natural to become frustrated and stop reacting. Indecision and inaction set in. It seems safer just to sit and wait out the storm.

Sitting and waiting out a storm, however, means that you could be aimlessly tossed about without control over your destiny. You may drift back toward shore or, worse, toward a swirling vortex that will spin you endlessly into oblivion.

Keep moving toward your goals and vision. You may topple a few times, but as long as you are moving toward your destination, you will reach it. It may not be as fast as you would like, but you will get there.

*I am action oriented and refuse to give up even when the
changes and challenges I face seem overwhelming.*

DAY 89

"*He who exercises government by means of his virtue may be compared to the north polar star, which keeps its place and all the stars turn towards it.*"

CONFUCIUS

*I*n these times of instability and insecurity the last thing people need is leaders who are themselves unstable. As a leader you have a tremendous responsibility to be the rock that people can rely on when everything else in their world may be falling apart.

You cannot control the outside environment. You cannot stop the wave of change that is sweeping into every aspect of life. You can, however, hold steadfastly to your own values and principles regardless of what is happening around you. It is the only way you can remain steady and provide a sense of stability to others. Identify clearly your values and principles. Share them with others. Then live them unfailingly for all to see.

Today I make a special effort to maintain my steadfastness of values and principles to create a sense of security and stability in my presence.

DAY 90

---○---

*"People are not an interruption of our business.
People are our business."*
WALTER E. WASHINGTON

No matter what we do we must consider the end user of our services, the customer. All forward-thinking organizations now realize the importance of serving the customer. Even organizations that have not traditionally believed that they had an end consumer, and therefore did not worry about serving anyone, now realize that their existence hinges on people.

No matter what you do, you have a constituency that justifies your position. Whether they are internal or external to your organization, without them you could not survive. Treat those who come to you with a service mentality. Live for them. Work for them. Serve them well, and they will guarantee your prosperity. Remember that the people you lead follow your example. Show them how important your customers are.

*I am constantly aware of the importance of customers in my life
and in my organization. I serve to the best of my ability
and encourage others to do the same.*

DAY 91

"Many receive advice, but only the wise profit by it."
PUBLILIUS SYRUS

*P*eople are always ready to offer their advice, whether we want it or not. Good leaders ask for it from anyone in a position to proffer information that will be helpful in the multitude of decisions they face daily. The strange thing about advice is how seldom people actually act upon it.

You need others to guide you and direct you just as much as others need you for the same reasons. Listen thoughtfully and carefully when you ask people for their insight. Take advantage of their experiences and collective wisdom.

Be careful not to involve too many people. Then you become confused and do not know who to believe. Choose carefully the advice you ask for. Then do something with it.

*I continually develop and improve the network of people
I can rely on when I need help making decisions.*

DAY 92

*"The idea that to make a man work you've got to hold
gold in front of his eyes is a growth, not an axiom.
We've done that for so long that we've forgotten
there's any other way."*

F. SCOTT FITZGERALD

*I*t is a common fallacy to believe that money is the primary
motivation of all people. Many studies have shown just
the opposite. In a survey of people who were unhappy with their
jobs, money was the number five reason they stated for being
dissatisfied. The number one reason was that their managers did
not communicate with them.

The people you lead want more than anything to feel important and to be treated with dignity. They want to be involved in
something bigger than both of you. They want vision. They want
meaning in their life and in their work. Of course they want
money, but money cannot replace the other value-based reasons
that people have for staying where they are. It is your responsibility to motivate them with your vision, your values, and your
respect for their own visions and values. If these things are aligned,
the people you lead will stay with you long after someone else
offers them a few dollars more to move.

*I am exceptional in my ability to motivate others
with my vision and values and at the same
time, treat them with respect and dignity.*

DAY 93

---

*"Next to knowing all about your own business, the best
thing is to know all about the other fellow's business."*
JOHN D. ROCKEFELLER

Competition grows increasingly more fierce with each
passing day. At one time anyone could count on developing a sustainable advantage over their competition that
would last for years. There was no real need to worry about what
was going on with them. There were unwritten rules to stay
out of each other's way—a sort of noncompetition by mutual
agreement.

Tighter economies and inexpensive new technologies have
changed the competitive environment. If you do not know what
is going on with your competition, you will be trampled. What
is their mission? What is their vision? What advantages do they
currently have or are they developing?

Knowing what your competitors are up to allows you the
advantage of predicting their next move or at least moving quickly
when they do. Remember to keep an eye out for new competitors. There is always someone new waiting in the wings to take
over when you take your eye off the ball.

*Today I will take meaningful action to learn more about
my competitors. I constantly monitor their actions
with an eye on assuring competitive advantage.*

DAY 94

---

*"Method goes far to prevent trouble in
business; for it makes the task easy,
hinders confusion, saves abundance
of time, and instructs those who
have business depending, what to
do and what to hope."*

WILLIAM PENN

*A*s important as they are, passion, focus, vision, and
principle are not the only factors for excellence.

Functional processes must also be in place for you to be able
to accomplish everything you aspire to. For every goal there must
be an action plan. It must be clear, highlighting dates and the
people responsible for each task's completion. A process has to
be put into place to regularly communicate your passion. You
have to have a measurement to be sure that you are completing
your values and principles.

It is easy to craft a pretty vision or mission statement. True
success comes with the hard work of developing the necessary
processes to be sure that the essence of your leadership converts
to tangible results.

*I consciously strive to have clear and functional
processes in place to assure that the essence
of my leadership is tangible.*

DAY
95

---

*"Keep away from people who try to belittle your ambitions.
Small people always do that, but the really great make
you feel that you, too, can become great."*
MARK TWAIN

*B*e aware of the people in your life who are not supporting you. They can be anywhere. Even those you are
closest to may fall victim to petty jealousies that can undermine
your success.

Once you identify people who are not supporting you, take
action immediately. Distance yourself from their slings and ar-
rows. Define new rules for the game.

You need people to reach your highest success. You cannot
afford to be around people who are not bolstering you. You have
so much to do, and time is short. Negative energy from others
translates into unconscious or conscious sabotage and results in
lost opportunities.

There are a lot of people who can see the value of your vision.
Target and recruit them. Their benevolence and greatness will
give you the positive energy you need to soar.

*I attract like-minded souls and mentors on the path to success.
Because of the strength of my purpose, they positively
support me and guide me on my journey.*

DAY 96

---

*"The best executive is the one who has sense enough
to pick good men to do what he wants done,
and self-restraint enough to keep from meddling
with them while they do it."*
THEODORE ROOSEVELT

*M*any leaders find it difficult to recruit people who are better or brighter than they are. It takes a great deal of security in your position to have someone superior on your crew. What if someone realizes your incompetence in one area or another?

You need people on your side who can fill in the gaps of your experience and knowledge. This was always the case, but it is becoming more evident as technology and speed change the way we transact business. Find people with skills and talents that complement your own. Then get out of the way. Demonstrate your confidence and competence by giving them the power to make decisions and get things done.

*I recruit only the brightest and the best. Their knowledge
and competence highlight my strengths and
demonstrate my keen abilities to lead.*

DAY 97

"The task of management is not to apply a formula but to decide issues on a case-by-case basis. No fixed, inflexible rule can ever be substituted for the exercise of sound business judgment in the decision-making process."
ALFRED P. SLOAN JR.

Strict rules are the by-product of an age when bureaucracy flourished. They work well when you need to control large groups of people who do not have the skills necessary to make decisions.

However, the days when workers were uneducated are ending. Organizations that allow information to filter throughout the system are excelling. Customization of products and working relationships has become the norm. In this environment, the people who make the organization work need to be able to evaluate the rules continually. They need to be empowered to change them when necessary to make the end customer happy and the organization efficient and profitable.

Lead in an empowering way. Teach others to be skeptical of the rules and bureaucracy that get in their way. Make sure that they have the skills necessary to carry out the analysis needed in your organization so that you manage processes and not policies.

I excel in my abilities to empower people to evaluate opportunities and circumvent any bureaucracy that gets in their way.

DAY
98

---

*"If money is your hope for independence you will never
have it. The only real security that a man
can have in this world is a reserve of
knowledge, experience, and ability."*

HENRY FORD

*P*eople used to choose a career for life. Things were
stable. Jobs were secure. There was no need to keep
up with the latest technology. It didn't change through the length
of a career. There was no need for accountability. Decisions were
made from above, and workers followed orders.

Now the work world is insecure. There is no job security.
Those who are taking advantage of learning opportunities to pol-
ish and advance their skills are discovering security. Even if the
job does not last, which few do, those with updated skills will
be secure in the marketplace.

Maintain skills so that you can maintain your position. Help
your team do the same. Your responsibility has moved from
making decisions to developing people. Continual learning is a
challenge that is rewarding and reflects the true essence of leadership.

*Today I will take action to assess where I need to develop so that I
can maintain the leading edge of my position. I continually
encourage learning on all levels of my team.*

DAY 99

"Empty barrels make the most noise."
E. M. WRIGHT

Where do you dedicate your attention and your forces amongst the people you encounter? If you are like many, the old saying "the squeaky wheel gets the grease" hits home. At home, in our professional lives, or in our friendships, the people who make the most commotion are not always the ones who provide us the most return on our investment of time and attention.

Analyze where you are spending your time and energy. Then look around at the people who tirelessly and silently support you and your efforts. Are you dedicating your attention sufficiently in their direction? They probably deserve more recognition than you are giving them. Find ways to show your appreciation. Find ways to be sure they have the tools they need to support your vision. Deal with the "squeaky wheels," but be sure to acknowledge the silent champions who tirelessly sustain you.

I will take action today to recognize those who silently and tirelessly support my efforts. Through their assistance I am able to succeed in my goals and dreams.

DAY
100

"The trouble with corporate America is that too many people with too much power live in a box (their home) and travel the same road every day to another box (their office)."

FAITH POPCORN

*H*uman beings are creatures of habit. In an insecure world, our habits give us a peace of mind, perhaps because we do not have to think about them. The problem with habits is that they become so comfortable we do not change, even when we know we should.

Are you doing the same things more out of habit than out of logic? What areas of your life could you improve if you only took a look from a different perspective? Evaluate your habits. They may not be effective anymore. Maybe they were never effective.

Find a new way to look at the world. Take a new road to work in the morning, talk to someone new during a coffee break, or enroll in a class outside of your current expertise. New horizons will open up if only you leave your box and see what is waiting out there for you to discover.

I will do something different today so that I can view the world from another perspective. New opportunities are waiting if I am willing to break old habits and try something new.

DAY
101

———○———

"When I can no longer create anything, I'll be done for."
COCO CHANEL

*L*eaders are constantly besieged by new problems and challenges. The tendency is to refer to experience and come up with a quick solution. No time is wasted. The leader can move on to the next challenge or get on with the daily workload. The same old solutions, based on experience, can lead back to the same old problems. Obstacles facing leaders today are new—the results of new technologies and new ways of doing business.

Be creative in your approach. Tom Peters talks about the need for leaders and organizations to be more "crazy." There is value in craziness. Few would argue that we are living in crazy times. Off-the-wall solutions work. Even if an idea is so off-the-wall that you could never use it, the thought might inspire a lasting systemic answer needed to keep the problem from continually resurfacing.

When faced with challenges, I avoid immediately turning
to the obvious solution based on experience.
I explore and encourage creative options
for today's "crazy" problems.

DAY
102

———◯———

"We only do well the things we like doing."
COLETTE

Who are the people in your circle you rely on to move your vision forward? Some of these people are probably doing exceptionally well, and some are surely foundering. Chances are that the ones who are prospering are working in areas where their talents are allowed to flourish. They are doing what they like. They are good at it. They are motivated.

What about the ones who are struggling? Are they toiling away in drudgery on projects they have no interest in? It may not be drudgery, but perhaps they are not performing well because they secretly, or not so secretly, dislike what they are doing. It is just a job.

Find ways to provide opportunities for people to feel fulfilled. People need to contribute their talents in ways that add value to the organization and add satisfaction to their lives. Work with them to combine their contribution and their talents. They will be more productive, happier, and more active in helping you.

I continually strive to encourage others to discover ways to use their unique talents to carry out their responsibilities.

DAY 103

---○---

*"Pioneers may be picturesque figures,
but they are often rather lonely ones."*
NANCY ASTOR

*B*eing a leader has many benefits. You are continually inspiring others and forging new ground. You paint the picture of the final destination. You clear the way and guide others over new paths toward frontiers they never would have dreamed possible. Others hold you up on a pedestal.

Who guides you, though? When you are the main source of inspiration, it can be tiring. Your energy motivates. Your drive keeps things moving. You are unique, which is why people follow you. There seldom is anyone to motivate you.

It can be a lonely journey when you are leading others. Find help and guidance in your own inner strength. Turn outward to find your own higher power to guide you. You will feel less lonely if you do so, and you will stay motivated so that you can encourage those who are relying on your direction.

*I am able to inspire myself to lead by turning inward
to my own unlimited power and energy, while also
relying on the strength and guidance that
come from my own higher power.*

DAY 104

---○---

"Life engenders life. Energy creates energy. It is by spending oneself that one becomes rich."
SARAH BERNHARDT

When you dedicate your life and work to a higher purpose, the energy needed to accomplish tasks associated with it seems unlimited. It pours forth like a summer rainstorm in the tropics. You are easily able to carry out your aspirations with enthusiasm and vigor.

Without a higher purpose the effort required to complete daily tasks is monumental. You procrastinate because you have no determination. Your heart just is not in it.

This is one of the challenges of life. Finding your higher purpose is instrumental to finding the intense power needed to accomplish great things. Settling for less than being passionate about your purpose relegates you to a foundering existence.

Work on finding your passion. Then link your passion to your work. It is the connection that energizes. It will continually build upon itself to help you to accomplish more than you dream possible.

I actively seek and find the connection between my work and a higher purpose that motivates me, giving me access to an endless supply of energy and vitality.

DAY
105

---○---

*"I am one of those people who just can't help getting a
kick out of life—even when it's a kick in the teeth."*
POLLY ADLER

*L*ife is truly funny. Even at its most tragic, if you look
for the humorous, you will find it. The human condition in all its frailty and brutality can be taken lightly when compared to the greater scale of things. It takes an open, sensitive
mind to look through the surface and see the irony below.

In our everyday condition there are joyful events happening
in conjunction with the tragic. There is slapstick where there is
frantic activity. There is heartwarming tenderness where there is
heart-wrenching disaster.

Of course we should feel for those injured in tragic circumstances. At the same time we should be open to the joys, laughter,
and inspiration found in the same situations. Looking at life too
seriously leads to bitterness and depression. Looking at the lighter
side adds balance and sanity to what could be a desperate life.

*My ability to see the balance between the tragic and the humorous
adds balance and sanity to my existence. Today I will make
a special effort to appreciate the lighter side of life.*

DAY 106

---○---

"The bitterest tears shed over graves are for words left unsaid and deeds left undone."
HARRIET BEECHER STOWE

*H*ow many times have you wished that you had shown your appreciation for a small act but things got in your way and then the time did not seem right? Our path to success is paved by the people who in big ways or in small helped us achieve our goals and vision. These same goals and vision get in our way when it comes to returning the deeds or showing appreciation. There is so much to be done, so little time to do it, and the burden for inspiring the vision rests on our shoulders. It is easy to find reasons to delay a good deed or an act of gratitude.

It is never too late to say a kind word of appreciation. Recognition is one of the greatest rewards you can bestow on someone who has helped you.

Say what you feel before it is too late. Return a good deed in good time. The goodwill generated by your acknowledgment of others' contributions to your success will pay them back a thousandfold.

Today I will take action to show my appreciation to someone who has contributed to my growth and success.

DAY 107

"The means by which we live have outdistanced the ends for which we live. Our scientific power has outrun our spiritual power. We have guided missiles and misguided men."

MARTIN LUTHER KING JR.

*T*here is a moral crisis in the world. The breakdown of the family is epidemic across all social and cultural boundaries. Many people are driven by a desire for instant gratification in spite of the long-term consequences.

People have become so accustomed to accessing immediate pleasure at a small short-term cost that they do not look at the long-term cost. It takes discipline to live up to a higher moral code. It takes energy and strength of character to maintain your principles.

You have an obligation to serve society in a special way. Set the example for others to follow. You set the long-term vision, the standards, the morality of your organization. With the end in mind, you know whether the means are justified. Your own discipline will become a model that others will feel obligated to follow. You must make the difference.

I am disciplined in my morality and steadfastly adhere to my principles no matter what the short-term cost or gain.

DAY 108

---

*"In the arena of human life the honors and rewards fall
to those who show their good qualities in action."*
ARISTOTLE

What are you doing to best utilize your own unique talents in order to accomplish your vision? All of us have talents that make us particularly capable in our positions. The problem is that few people fully utilize their talents.

Identify what your talents are. What is your own area of genius? In what ways can you fully apply your gifts in order to realize your objectives? These questions sound simple, but many implications arise as a result of asking them. If you are not fully utilizing your abilities, ask yourself why.

We are most effective when we take action with our talents in a way that contributes to our success and to the success of others. Take steps today to actively use your innate capacities to further your development and the progression of your vision.

*I have many unique talents that I am motivated to utilize
in the pursuit of my vision. I take action today to identify
them and actively use them to further my progression.*

DAY 109

---○---

"In helping others to succeed we insure our own success."
WILLIAM FEATHER

*H*ave you mapped out your path to success? If you have, you have certainly realized how important other people are to the accomplishment of your goals and aspirations. It is not only that you cannot reach your pinnacle without others but also that you would not even have a standard by which to measure your success.

What are you doing to help others succeed? As part of your own plan for growth, include a plan to help others. Whether they are more advanced than you, at your level, or just starting to climb the ladder to success, people in your life need your help to achieve their desires. The more ways you find to assist them, the greater the chances that you will be swept into their current. You will flow along together managing to triumph over any obstacles that get in your way.

I am always on the lookout for opportunities to help others succeed. Through their success, my own success happens controllably and effortlessly.

DAY 110

*"Good management consists of showing average people
how to do the work of superior people."*
JOHN D. ROCKEFELLER

*T*he rewards for leaders have changed. It used to be that leaders were rewarded for having all the answers. If there was a fire to be put out, the one who could put it out the fastest and most effectively was applauded as a hero. It feels good to be the one with all the solutions there to share with anyone in a bind.

In the new world it is impossible to possess all the information. Without adequate information, it is impossible to douse the flames of organizational fires that pop up faster than ever. Leaders who develop their people and help them learn to succeed on their own are the ones who will be the new heroes. Through helping others succeed and be their own heroes your own status will rise to immeasurable heights.

*I am an excellent problem solver, and much of my success
has been the result of my abilities. My future lies in
helping others learn to do what I do best.*

DAY 111

*"In any given society the authority of man over man
runs in inverse proportion to the intellectual
development of that society."*
PIERRE-JOSEPH PROUDHON

*I*n spite of the worries in the general population over
illiteracy and falling school standards, people in the workforce are more educated and experienced than ever before. This
change has profound impact on the way leaders manage people
and help their organizations to grow.

Managers used to give orders, and those below them jumped
to it. No questions. No delay. It was assumed that the leader
had more education, information, and experience than the person being directed. That assumption has gone away, and with it
is going the top-down autocratic style.

Find ways to manage others by giving them the information
they need to effectively accomplish their tasks, and wide enough
parameters for making decisions. These are the conditions necessary to get a more educated and experienced populace to work
happily and effectively. They do not take orders anymore, and
we cannot afford to lose their skills.

*In many ways the people I lead are more informed and experienced
than I am. Today I will concentrate on taking advantage of their
skills and giving them the leeway they need to be effective.*

DAY 112

---○---

"Modesty is what ails me. That's what's kept me under."
ARTEMUS WARD

*W*e grow up being told that it is not becoming to brag about ourselves and our accomplishments. Modesty is supposed to be the best approach. We admire the blushing demeanor of humble role models as they are honored for their achievements or asked about the secret of their success.

That same humility can get in the way of your progress along the path to success. As the saying goes, if you do not toot your own horn, who will? An army does not vanquish an enemy without returning heroically to its nation to triumphantly announce victory. Nations rejoice in being saved. The vanquished learn to be more careful where they tread.

Announce your victories from the highest treetop. Let others see how high you have soared. Respect and advancement come easily to those who let others know their qualifications.

I am victorious in many endeavors and proudly announce
my accomplishments so that others will be aware
of the value of my skills and abilities.

DAY 113

"Having principles is easier than living up to them."
ARNOLD GLASOW

*C*hances are you have attended some sort of conference, meeting, or training that spoke of the importance of having values and living a principled life. Maybe you have explored your own principles through one of these meetings or in your house of worship. Perhaps you have read one of the multitude of books that expound the importance of principles. Everyone seems to be talking about them. It would be hard to argue against principles and values.

All the talk about integrity is accompanied by the belief that our morals and ethics are on a downhill slide. You may not be able to personally stop the decline in moral values, but your example will inspire. Continually define and live your principles. Forgo short-term satisfaction if the satisfaction means you have to compromise your own principles. Your advancement along a principled path may be just the encouragement others need to bravely do the same, even if it is at cross-purposes with their immediate desires and the direction of society.

*I consistently live my morality and principles. My example
is an inspiration to others and together we can
change the direction of the world.*

DAY 114

---○---

"The world belongs to the energetic."
RALPH WALDO EMERSON

People are forever looking for potions and formulas to provide unlimited energy. From the snake oils of the Old West to the vitamin pills with iron of today, we try to find easy ways to get more energy. There is a simple way to be more energetic. You do not need a doctorate in vitamin supplement therapy. It is not necessarily easy, however, and that is the catch.

The most energetic people are the ones who eat well, exercise, and maintain a normal weight level. People who feel that they are contributing to a higher cause often feel the most energetic. Sometimes it seems that the effort to exercise and eat right is not worth it. In the long run, these few things pay off in more stamina and vigor than you could hope for. Pay attention to your body and your mental attitude. If your body is in top condition and you are careful about what you use to fuel it (both physically and mentally), it will reward you with all the energy you need to accomplish your goals and enjoy the fruits of your labor.

Today I will adjust my schedule to be sure I am making enough room for physical activity and eating well. I am more energetic with each purposeful day that passes.

DAY 115

*D*id you ever feel as if you spilt forth too much by opening your big mouth? Of course you have. Everyone says things he or she regrets or speaks in a way that is hurtful more for the delivery than for the message. Leaders cannot afford to have this happen very often. Communication is the means by which you accomplish everything. People rely on you for the best feedback or information in the most appropriate manner.

Weigh exactly how the message will be perceived before you say anything. Even if what you have to say seems of little consequence, bad timing or misunderstandings can have a profound negative effect on the person with whom you are communicating. Your message will gain greater clarity and impact when you give it the time to develop in your mind before it leaves your mouth.

I endeavor to be recognized as an excellent communicator. I weigh my words carefully for the right meaning and impact before I say them to others.

DAY 116

"Discovery consists of looking at the same thing as everyone else and thinking something different."
ALBERT SZENT-GYÖRGYI

Who could have guessed that there was a latent demand for little yellow pads that could stick to things and be removed easily? Who would have thought that the world would beat a path to buy computers and phones they could take with them to the beach or on camping trips in the wilderness? If you had asked consumers to tell you their needs, they would not have even imagined these items.

Someone imagined them. Someone looked at the world and saw a need that few would ever have conceived. The people who saw these things were no brighter or more imaginative than their co-workers. They just had an ability to see opportunity in the world around them. They used what they saw around them to create something new, something just different enough, that everyone had to have it.

You have that ability too. Look around you. Where are the needs? Use what you have at your disposal to fulfill those needs. Watch for the opportunities that always exist, then act on them. You are in a position to change the world.

I make it a point to identify opportunities, find creative ways to fulfill them, and have a positive impact on the world as a result.

DAY 117

"No man is an island, entire of itself; every man is a piece of the continent."

JOHN DONNE

Where do you fit into the whole? You are really a cog in the great machine of human aspirations. Knowing where you fit and what your function is helps you outline your vision in a realistic and synergistic manner.

If your ideas do not fit into the grand scheme, they will not work. It does not help to try to push them through because no matter what you do, outside forces will prevent your progress. Take some time and analyze the overall picture. See where you have opportunities to go faster than you are or where you need to proceed more slowly. Figure out who is affected by your vision and how you can make it help them accomplish their vision. Your small part will pull together seamlessly and effortlessly if you find ways to coordinate with the greater whole.

I continually measure my vision and progress in terms of the effect on the greater whole and take steps to create synergy at all times.

DAY 118

---○---

*"Once we are destined to live out our lives in the prison
of our mind, our one duty is to furnish it well."*
PETER USTINOV

You are the only person who truly knows what is going on in your mind. Others may try to read you, but they will never know all the secret thoughts, aspirations, and drives that make your life move forward. What people can know, however, is your actions. Your thoughts, no matter how well you think they are hidden, drive your behavior.

Be sure that what you are allowing into your thoughts is worthy of your mission and of your dreams. Be careful of negative self-talk. If your internal conversations are downbeat while you attempt to project outward signs of confidence, others will easily read through the bravado and perceive what is going on inside. Keep your thoughts wholesome and consistent with your dreams and the appearance you want to project to the world.

*My inner thoughts influence the appearance I project,
so I continually strive for thoughts to support
my dreams and aspirations.*

DAY 119

---

*"Nothing that can be can come between me
and the full prospect of my hopes."*
WILLIAM SHAKESPEARE,
TWELFTH NIGHT, ACT 3, SCENE 4

*S*ome days it seems as if everything gets in your way. Your plans are interrupted by telephone calls, E-mail messages, and computers. People take up your time and your energy with petty problems. The day ends before you even have a chance to accomplish everything on your list—maybe even before you have the chance to make up a list.

On some days when you cannot seem to do anything but tread water, you may feel that you are not progressing toward any of your visions or goals. When you feel an invisible force pushing you back from your dreams, you may want to quit. In reality, these things are minor as long as you do not let them take your focus off your plans. Keep focused. Look ahead for the light at the end of the tunnel. As long as you have a clear picture in your mind of where you are going, you will not have to worry about the minor, or even major, setbacks along the way.

*I keep my sights set on a clear vision. Each and every day I review
and refocus that vision so that I can maintain my positive
attitude and belief in accomplishing it.*

DAY 120

---

*"You may be deceived if you trust too much, but you will
live in torment if you don't trust enough."*

FRANK CRANE

*I*t takes a great leap of faith to trust others. It is a faith
that is hard to have, because if we are honest with ourselves, we know that we should not always be fully trusted either.
Our intentions are not always as positive as others might believe.
We have our own secret agendas and hidden plans. Sometimes
we hold back information in order to further our own interests.

If this is the case, how can you trust others? In truth, you
have no choice. There is only so much you can do before you
have to rely on the expertise and talents of other people. Inherent
in that reliance is a need to trust them to live as closely as possible
to your expectations. The most important factors in a trusting
relationship are communication and expectations. If expectations
are clear and you communicate when you have doubts and when
you are satisfied, your own trust level will build. Finally, use good
judgment and then have faith. You need others. Trust that they
will do their best for you.

*Today I will be more trusting. I have faith that I can trust people
when I am clear about the expectations and maintain open
communication of the good and the bad.*

DAY 121

---○---

"The greater the difficulty, the greater the glory."
CICERO

Wouldn't it be nice if everything in life came easily? If only life were like a television show where there is no problem that cannot be solved in a half-hour or one-hour time block.

Of course life is not as easy as the television shows make it out to be. On television no one ever suffers through long hours of anticipation while waiting on approval for a project. On television it would seem that the chances of winning the lottery are favorable. In real life it is better to forget the lottery and get down to the plan for the hard work and struggle necessary to reach your goals. In real life, pain and tears are associated with any vision. If your goals are compelling and motivating enough, the pain will not seem bad compared with the pleasure of the end result.

It is normal that I am impatient, and much of the environment I live in reinforces that feeling. For that reason, I incessantly endeavor to see the value in patience and meticulous hard work.

DAY 122

---○---

*"Revolutions are like the most noxious dung-heaps,
which bring into life the noblest vegetables."*
NAPOLÉON BONAPARTE

*A*ll the change that everyone in the world is living with can be disconcerting. People like habits and strive to maximize their comfort and minimize pain and risk. Even those who are excited about change have difficulty with the massive amounts of change we are now forced to adapt to.

While we pass through the changes, be particularly aware of the human toll they take. There is no sense of security. People lose their jobs. Entire specialties disappear. Remember the hole punch operators of not so many years ago? What was to be the career of the future does not even exist today.

You can alleviate the uncertainty and anxiety by keeping a firm vision of the outcome. You can help others see not only the inevitability but also the benefits of the revolution of lifestyle and work we are facing. Your example on the forefront of change will inspire others to bravely attack new challenges and live their lives in animated expectation of what the new world will be.

*I have a unique ability to see the good hidden in the revolution we
call change. I use that vision to help others to see the possibilities
that changes have to positively affect their lives.*

DAY 123

"My philosophy is that not only are you responsible for your life, but doing the best at this moment puts you in the best place for the next moment."

OPRAH WINFREY

When you do something particularly well, it is easy to become somewhat lazy and not put forth your best effort at all times. You might save your best for when you know you are being observed by someone who can make a difference. You never know who is present in a crowd. It may be no one who could ever have an influence on your life, or it could be the one person who could launch you toward your dreams faster than you ever imagined.

Do your personal best at all times no matter what the task. Do not fall into the trap of doing a mediocre job when you think no one will notice. It is always noticed, if not for the mediocrity then for the inconsistency. Let others know the importance of doing their own personal best and form an expectation of unwavering excellence every step of the way.

Today I will make it a point to perform at my personal best, no matter who is paying attention. My insistence on excellence carries through to everyone I deal with.

DAY 124

---

*"A man can succeed at anything for which
he has unlimited enthusiasm."*

CHARLES M. SCHWAB

*A*re you passionate enough about what you are doing?
Does your enthusiasm for your vision and your goals
spark the flame of excitement everywhere you touch? Successful
people are always enthusiastic people. I would bet you have
seldom met someone who is truly successful speak in a monotone
about their life purpose or the completion of their mission.

Choose your dreams carefully. Sustained success comes from
having a calling and acting upon it with vigor. Do what you love.
Breathe it. Study it. Talk it. You will find that doing what you
love will bring you the kind of true success you are searching for.
The decorations of money, fame, and security do not come on
their own. They are the resultant outcropping of taking action
on your passions.

*I have a calling. Today I will invest time thinking about
my passions and take action to be sure that I am
living them enthusiastically and energetically.*

DAY 125

"Some men see things as they are and say 'Why?' I dream things that never were and say 'Why not?'"
ROBERT F. KENNEDY

T he world is yours to dream it however you wish. That is a bold statement. Some would look around and point out why it is not true. They would say you cannot eliminate certain aspects of society that would prevent their real dreams from being carried forth. They might say that things are the way they are because that is the way they were created by God.

The reality is that many of society's ills have been eliminated or reduced because people had dreams. Only recently could the average person expect to live longer than forty years. Now medical advances have increased our life expectancies and quality. Many feudal systems of oppression have given way. Things have come a long way. There is still a long way to go, but the earth is infinitely more inhabitable and comfortable for the average person than ever. You can do your part to make it even better. You can dream elimination of injustices, sicknesses, famine. Dream it. Then do it.

I can turn my dreams for a more just, disease-free, well-fed world into realities. Today I will begin doing just a little bit more to make it happen faster.

DAY 126

"People should think things out fresh and not just accept conventional terms and the conventional way of doing things."
BUCKMINSTER FULLER

NIHS. Not Invented Here Syndrome has been a common way of doing business in many organizations for years. The mentality that there is nothing to be learned from the outside or from new ways of thinking has sent many organizations to their graves. Organizations need to constantly check themselves and their processes to see what new things they can do to get better.

Continuous improvement is the survival mechanism for organizations in the ultra-competitive arena. It means constantly examining what you are doing and how you are doing it, and making necessary changes. Even if the changes are painful, you have to insist on them. The marketplace will not allow stagnant organizations to survive, regardless of how just their cause or how long they have been around. Keep up your program of continuous improvement and keep up your chances of surviving in turbulent times.

I regularly stimulate the process of continuous improvement in my organization. Even if it is painful at times, it assures our survival and prosperity.

DAY 127

"Diamonds are only chunks of coal,
That stuck to their jobs, you see."
MINNIE RICHARD SMITH

*P*ersistence is a value often overlooked in terms of importance. The rewards in our society seem to come from instant success. We often develop that belief because we read about many people whose success seemed to happen instantaneously. Theirs are the stories published in the newspapers and trumpeted by the anchors of the news magazine shows.

Did you ever wonder why lottery winners and flash business successes hit the press? It is because they are so rare. If success were as instantaneous for everyone as it is for the few profiled in stories, then it would cease to become news. Actually, the person who toils daily, working hard and directed toward a vision, is more often than not the one who will achieve a sustainable success.

Work diligently toward your goals. Do not pay attention to the quick success of others. Do not give up until you know you have exhausted all avenues to your success, then do so only as a last resort. Perseverance pays.

I have the ability to make my perseverance legendary.
My success comes from purposefully and patiently
working to achieve my dreams.

DAY 128

---○---

"Make yourself a seller when you are buying,
and a buyer when you are selling, and
then you will sell and buy justly."
ST. FRANCIS DE SALES

*W*e are taught to live life by the Golden Rule: Do unto others as you would have them do unto you. This rule only goes so far. Taking it a step further, perhaps it would be a good idea to live life according to this rule: Do unto others as they would have *you* do unto *them*.

A key to selling something, whether a product, an idea, or a vision, is the ability to empathize. You must see things as the other person sees them. You must feel things as they feel them deep within their hearts. Put yourself into the other person's place and develop an idea of what the product, idea, or vision means for them. Only in this way can you position your proposal in a way that is appealing to them. They will only buy from you if they feel you have their needs in account and are acting in their benefit.

As a leader, I am in the business of selling ideas. I remember to constantly use empathy as a tool to understand the impact and benefits of my ideas on others' lives.

DAY 129

*"Mistrust a subordinate who never finds
fault with his superior."*
JOHN CHURTON COLLINS

*T*he world is full of "yes men." Look around you. It is astounding how many leaders surround themselves with people who tell them only what they want to hear. No one likes his or her ideas contradicted. Leaders are especially vulnerable to the temptation of listening only to those who are always in agreement. Perhaps it is because of the need to have people on board who can follow a vision as passionately as the leader does.

There is a difference between having people who follow your vision and people who never disagree with you. Competent associates will tell their leader when they are exposed to possible pitfalls. They will object when pushed in a direction that jeopardizes the dream. Do not fall into the comfort zone of constant agreement. Look for people who will bravely argue with you. Insist on the truth at every turn. The survival of your vision is at stake.

*I will take steps today to encourage truth from all my associates,
even if it is painful and I do not want to hear it. The future
of my vision is always my prime consideration.*

DAY
130

---○---

"A company cannot increase its productivity. People can."
ROBERT HALF

*D*ownsizing. Rightsizing. Decreasing headcount. They all indicate the same thing. The old social contract that guaranteed jobs for life is unraveling around the world. This has profound implications for leaders as they attempt to balance shifting economies and skill needs with the need for humanity and creation of opportunity.

In the short run, cutting expenses by cutting labor may seem like a better idea than it really is. If the shift means that everyone left will have to work unceasingly with no hope for a secure position you may lose the productivity you hope to gain.

If you are going to downsize, examine all processes that need changing. Be sure they are changed and that there are no pockets that are protected by special interests or hidden agendas. Do not make five people do the same amount of work that ten used to do. Persist in looking at the way the work is done as well as at who is doing the work.

People make our products and services the best
available. I continually take steps to be sure
that the processes are modern and in pace
with our productivity resources.

DAY 131

---○---

*"Work expands so as to fill the time
available for its completion."*
C. NORTHCOTE PARKINSON

*T*hink about how much work you completed the day
before you last took a vacation. Why is it that we
can accomplish so much under pressure, yet when we have a lot
of time for preparation it is so easy to put things off? Even worse,
if we do start to work on a project early into the cycle, it seems
as if we spend more time coming up with the same result than
if we had waited until the last minute.

Much of the problem lies in an inherent need for perfectionism. If we have a lot of time to complete an activity, it
increases our feelings that the outcome should be faultless. Some
tasks require completely flawless execution. I would not want to
fly in a plane that was not in perfect working condition. That
does not mean that mechanics have all the time in the world to
work on a plane. They are under extreme time pressures. They
still manage to perfectly execute their tasks. Strive for excellence
at all times but do not let perfectionism get in the way of the
efficient execution of projects and tasks.

*I strive for excellence, but I do not let
perfectionism get in the way.*

DAY 132

*"The louder he talked of his honor,
the faster we counted our spoons."*
RALPH WALDO EMERSON

*T*here is something to be said for quiet understatement. One of the fastest ways to draw suspicion regarding your intentions is to state them forthrightly too many times. Values and principles are meant to be lived. Many believe that to make up for not living them as faithfully as they should, they can repeat them to anyone who will listen. This tactic is as transparent as an Adirondack lake.

Live your principles. Do quietly what you might be tempted to announce. You will find that everyone will know you live a principled life. You will never have to draw their attention to it. Avoid announcing values that you have no intention of living, even though you believe in them. Your own actions will reveal the hypocrisy of your ways, and all the trumpeting in the world will not cover it up.

*I quietly endeavor to live my principles in all aspects of my life.
Through my actions I inspire others to a principled lifestyle.*

DAY 133

---○---

*"The body has its own way of knowing, a knowing that
has little to do with logic, and much to do with truth,
little to do with control, and much to do with
acceptance, little to do with division and
analysis, and much to do with union."*
MARILYN SEWELL

*L*eaders have more data at their fingertips than they know what to do with. You can run computerized analyses of forecast metrics in any format. You can push and pull the statistics in any way to squeeze out any report.

No amount of information can take all the risks out of a decision. You can learn the skills you need to analyze data in any number of ways, but you cannot learn how to use your intuition. It comes with experience. It comes with trusting your own instincts and abilities to penetrate through to the unconscious and reach a conclusion based on feeling. As more information pervades our environment, it is even more important for you to develop your abilities to sense the meanings behind the numbers. Believe in yourself. You are capable of much more than you would logically think.

*Today I focus toward capitalizing on my intuition and unconscious
abilities to analyze information and make decisions.*

DAY 134

---◦---

*T*he world you lead is more openly diverse than ever in history. It has not been that long since blacks in the South were relegated to separate drinking fountains and the back of the bus. Only recently have opportunities opened for women and minorities to move into the upper ranges of the corporate hierarchies in the United States.

Diversity opens many new and unique challenges and opportunities for leaders. New interpersonal skills are required to understand people of different cultures, backgrounds, and lifestyles and help them to come together effectively. Leaders help this process by insisting on erasing old assumptions. Encouraging people to discover their similarities while treasuring their differences will bring new life and ideas into any situation. Question yourself. What assumptions are you holding that are no longer valid? Capitalize on the diversity that is available to you. Different outlooks and points of view add great value to your future.

*Today I will take action to add more diversity to my life
and leadership, whether by learning more about it,
mentoring someone, or challenging my previous
assumptions about people's roles.*

DAY 135

"Innovators are inevitably controversial."
EVA LE GALLIENNE

*O*ne of the greatest fears that humans experience is the fear of rejection. It translates in our psyches into the belief that those who reject us do not like us personally. Most people have a need to be liked. As a result, they may agree with things that they are opposed to. They may not stand up readily against the tide if their ideas are unpopular.

You must be innovative. By being so, you risk ruffling the feathers of a lot of birds who are comfortable with the status quo. Any innovation will bring controversy. There will always be those who disagree with you. Disagreement and rejection of your ideas have more to do with their self-interests than your personality. Let them go. Stand for your beliefs. Even though not everyone will agree, no one will be able to fault you for standing by your principles.

I am an innovator and incessantly endeavor to find
more effective ways to do things. Even though I may
be controversial, others respect me for
my principled stance on the issues.

DAY 136

Carpe diem. Seize the day. The words sizzle with truth. If you have a dream, act on it today. If you have a vision, take steps to bring it to reality now. You never know what tomorrow will bring.

Once you take action on your visions and your dreams, you will find that corresponding opportunities will crystallize. It is one thing to think about doing things. It is quite another to do what is necessary to make them happen. You have all the resources you need to make your dreams happen now. Things do not get easier the longer you wait. If you miss the window of opportunity by not taking action, you could miss your dream. It could evaporate before you even know it is gone.

*I will immediately seize the opportunity to take action
on an unrealized dream. Through my action,
great things will come to pass.*

DAY 137

---○---

*"If we would have new knowledge, we must
get a whole world of new questions."*
SUSANNE K. LANGER

*T*he quality of the questions you ask dictates the quality of the answers you receive. So many questions we ask of ourselves and others are not really questions. We tend to state affirmations as questions. We want a certain answer, so we state a closed-ended question in a way that will get us the answer we want. Questions like "You don't want to do that now, do you?" do nothing except help the asker feel as if we let someone participate in a decision and tell the person the response we want.

Be especially careful of this kind of behavior. Because of your unique position, others look for cues from you before taking stands. It may be good for your ego to lead them on with affirmation-style questions, but it will not give you information you need to adequately make decisions. Ask open-ended questions that will give you insight.

*I am acutely aware of the power of insightful questioning. I will
work toward continually asking quality questions in order to
increase my understanding of areas critical to my success.*

DAY 138

———o———

*"Farming looks mighty easy when your plow is a pencil,
and you're a thousand miles from a corn field."*
DWIGHT D. EISENHOWER

*I*t used to be the norm for leaders to be responsible for a certain segment in a certain region. They were able to be intimately familiar with all aspects of their operation.

Now it is more the norm for leaders to be responsible for states, countries, and continents. It may sound like an easy jump from leading a region to leading in the international arena, but all sorts of new aspects come into play. Doing business with different cultures when you have never experienced them is a particularly difficult challenge. Add in doing it in a language you cannot speak and you have the basis for a formidable task, even for the most experienced leader.

As you face working in areas where you have no experience, take the time to learn what you can. Most of the time, your lack of knowledge in a certain area does not cause resentment and misunderstandings. What bothers people is lack of positive intent. Be prepared. If you are not already in this situation, you will soon be.

*I am doing all I can to prepare for the expansion
of my leadership into new areas. My positive
intent is sincere and obvious.*

DAY 139

*I*f you are using your talents, you are guaranteed more happiness and more success. It does not matter what your talents are, when you enjoy what you are doing you are likely to be more productive. In fact, your talents have probably gotten you where you are right now.

What about your associates? Are they being permitted to use their talents? Do you know what their talents are? Just as you are more likely to be happier and more productive when you are maximizing the use of your talents, your associates will be also. They, too, should feel that they are living their vocation rather than just doing their job. It is your responsibility to assess what their talents are and help them find ways to utilize those talents. Their satisfaction will increase, and they will reward you with more productivity.

I will take time today to assess my talents and those of my associates. I will take action to assure that we are all maximizing the use of our talents.

DAY 140

"He that would govern others, first should be the master of himself."

PHILIP MASSINGER

Self-mastery is one of the precepts of effective leadership. You cannot expect to help others master their actions and values if you are not master over your own. Like anything, this is easier said than done. If you do not live up to your own expectations of yourself, you will be the first to notice, and the hypocrisy creates a form of self-loathing that will disrupt your performance.

Keep the promises you make to yourself before anything else. Master your desires and impulses. Continually ask yourself if your actions are aligned with your principles. If they are not, then you must find new actions. There are no compromises when it comes to integrity. You either have it and act on it or you do not. You want to be the kind of leader that others respect. More than anything else, however, you want to maintain your own self-respect at all costs.

I am the master of my own principles and values, and I live them with the highest level of integrity. My own self-respect is more important than the recognition of anyone else.

DAY 141

*"Compared to what we ought to be, we are only half
awake. We are making use of only a small part
of our physical and mental resources."*

WILLIAM JAMES

*I*t is a well-known fact that we use only a small portion
of our brain. Most researchers agree that the maximum
utilization is 8 to 10 percent. It is phenomenal what we are able
to accomplish by using so little of our possible power.

You can increase your own abilities. For example, most people
develop their primary talents but leave secondary talents off to
the side because they take hard work. If you have an aptitude in
a certain area, use it.

Physically we tend to rely on only one primary modality of
perception. We are either visually, auditorily, or kinesthetically
oriented. Develop other prime receptors. If you are visually talented, spend some time learning to listen or learning to build
through doing. You can develop the cerebral connections to open
up your resources to new levels. Exercise your physical and mental
reserves. If you do not, they will atrophy and die.

*I am aware that there are physical and mental areas in which I can
develop. Today I will take action to develop new areas so that
I can continue my growth as a productive leader.*

DAY
142

———○———

*"Conversation means being able to disagree
and still continue the discussion."*
DWIGHT MACDONALD

*T*rue communication hinges on our willingness to talk
about sensitive topics in an honest and forthright manner. If you want your associates to perform at their peak, encourage them to disagree with you when it is necessary. They should
not only disagree with you but with each other as well.

There is a tremendous amount of fear associated with challenging others. Instead, what we develop is a culture of politeness.
When it comes to honestly questioning someone's premises and
asserting a controversial outlook, we smile and keep our thoughts
to ourselves. This is destructive behavior, even though it intuitively feels safe.

Insist that people feel safe when confronting. Lead with your
own example. Be courageous and confront when necessary and
encourage the members of your team to do the same with you.
Confrontive conversation is caring—and more effective—than polite repartee any day.

○

*I am able to confront even the most difficult person when I am right
and it is for the best. I actively encourage my team members
to feel safe to do the same with me and each other.*

DAY 143

---○---

"Man is not on the earth solely for his own happiness.
He is there to realize great things for humanity."
VINCENT VAN GOGH

What are you working for? If you are like many people, you are so overwhelmed by the demands of
your position that you spend most of your time working just to
get a day off. You spend the leftover energy on your own personal
satisfaction. When you get a little leisure you enjoy it relaxing,
visiting friends, eating, or watching a little television.

There is more to life than chasing the biggest buck and working
to create your own happiness. People who are gifted with leadership abilities have a responsibility to share their talents in service
to others. By serving humanity in some form you are actually
serving yourself. The energy recharge you get from helping improve an area you are passionate about more than makes up for
the energy spent. Choose a cause; then work for it. You have to
give back. It is part of the contract for the talents you have been
privileged to receive.

I am privileged to have been given many talents,
and in return, I serve humanity.

DAY 144

---○---

*A*re you dedicating your energies in the pursuit of success, or are you spending your energies trying to avoid failure? This is a fundamental question that all leaders must ask themselves. No one likes to fail. The disappointment and embarrassment can be debilitating for many, especially for those with big egos. Admit it: Like most leaders, you have a big ego.

How do you get over the failure complex then? Start by seeing each failure as an opportunity to learn. If you succeeded in everything you did on the very first attempt, you would have no basis for what success feels or looks like. You would not even know that you had succeeded. You acquire new skills only by understanding the dynamics of why they work. That usually happens when you grasp the consequences of not applying the skill. When you get it wrong, you have the opportunity to evaluate what you can do to be better the next time. You get the chance to improve on your style or design. Celebrate failure. Through it you will understand success.

I understand the need for failure in learning to succeed. I celebrate failures by learning everything I can from them and applying the knowledge gained.

DAY 145

"Inspiration is the impact of a fact on a prepared mind."
LOUIS PASTEUR

Where does inspiration come from? We deceive ourselves into thinking that it comes from the ether. We only need to sit out under the stars, open our minds, and breathe deeply. If we do this, the heavens will open and fill our brains with the most wondrous enlightenment, sending forth sparks of creativity and energy that will light the world on fire with our new ideas.

Inspiration takes a good deal more work and preparation than that. It takes awareness. It takes a keen eye for observing what is going on around you. Inspiration is really an idea for what to do with an opportunity. Before you can have inspiration, therefore, you have to have seen the opportunity. That comes only with constant vigilance. Scan the newspaper. Scan magazines. Scan conversations. This is where you will find the opportunities that will inspire you to act.

I am an expert at identifying opportunities. Through this ability
I am able to find inspiration to act on the possibilities
and motivate others to act also.

DAY 146

---

*"The drops of rain make a hole in the stone
not by violence but by oft falling."*

LUCRETIUS

*I*n the animal kingdom, the lion with the loudest roar gets the most attention. Is it really the most effective? The lion leads by fear and intimidation. The other habitants run and hide when they hear the roar. Have you known leaders with the same style? They bellow the loudest in an effort to get their way, intimidating all in their path. They believe their thunderous style can move mountains, but what it really does is move people away from them to hide in fear.

Gentle, consistent persuasion is what moves people. Leaders with unwavering vision who tenaciously work toward its completion are the ones who prevail. Persistence moves mountains. Tangible vision moves people. If you have both, you need never fear that people will hide from helping you succeed.

*I work to assure that my compelling vision is tangible and
motivating for all who follow my dream. Together
with tenacity, we can attain great heights.*

DAY 147

---○---

*"During my eighty-seven years I have witnessed a whole
succession of technological revolutions. But none of
them has done away with the need for character
in the individual or the ability to think."*
BERNARD M. BARUCH

*L*eaders are beginning to face a crisis of phenomenal
proportions. Where will they find the skilled people
to work in an increasingly technological and information-driven
environment?

Visionary leaders are acting now to fulfill future needs by creating learning organizations. Learning organizations help people acquire the skills and knowledge they need to effectively accomplish their mission. They are seeing the benefits of investing in people, the ultimate resource.

Invest in your people. Train them. Be sure they have the skills to survive in the age of technology and information. Do it for them, yes, but most of all do it for your organization. You will not survive without qualified humans no matter how smart the machines are.

*Today I will assess the needs of the people who rely on me to help
them develop. I will be sure we all have opportunities
for growth by stimulating a learning culture.*

DAY 148

*"There is only one rule for being a
good talker, learn to listen."*
CHRISTOPHER MORLEY

*T*he best conversationalist is usually the person who
says the least. Great conversationalists have learned
the most important skill to dialogue—listening. Many people say
they listen, but few actually become skilled at it. Mostly they
hear what others say and process it only so far as to develop their
own response.

The best listeners are empathetic. They listen as though they
were the person talking. They try to learn from the conversation.
They ask questions rather than respond. They are quick to release
when someone interrupts. More than just hearing someone's
message, they work to understand their meaning.

Labor to listen. By actively trying to understand your associates, you will have the tools to motivate them to discover the
direction you want them to take. They will do it by themselves
but think you spelled it out for them. And they will say you are
the gentlest person at giving direction that they have ever met.

*I am an exceptional listener. I listen to learn from others and
constantly work to understand their meaning, which gives
me the information I need to motivate them to excellence.*

DAY 149

---○---

"Laughter is inner jogging."
NORMAN COUSINS

*T*here are few doubts about the benefits of laughter on the human system. Laughter releases stress. It releases internal chemicals and hormones that provide a feeling of happiness and security. Laughter helps prevent sickness and has been proven to fight off infection and sickness. Laughter not only benefits the human system, but it helps the work system as well.

What are you doing to encourage laughter among those with whom you work? As pressures increase the tendency is to become more serious. People put their noses to the grindstone. Think of the image that conjures up. How about a laughter break once in a while? A little silliness will go a long way toward reducing tension. Lightheartedness will increase the creativity in your organization. If you encourage laughter and frivolity, others will join you, taking a welcome break from the tension. They will be motivated to accomplish their tasks with a sense of joy when they return to their senses.

I understand fully the healthful benefits of silliness and laughter. I make it a point to encourage a lighter attitude in the pursuit of our critical tasks and goals.

DAY 150

"We die on the day when our lives cease to be illuminated by the steady radiance, renewed daily, of a wonder, the source of which is beyond all reason."
DAG HAMMARSKJÖLD

When was the last time you watched a sunset? Not just noticed its orange splash across the concrete horizon as you drove home from work, but really watched it. Sunsets are magical. Their colorful show changes every night, yet their inevitability is as unchanging as time itself. They are the last stroke of beauty that the earth paints for us before the black and white enchantment of the night sky starts its twinkling show.

No wonder, then, that whenever humankind has searched for a sense of spirituality our sights have turned to the skies. Heavenward. We mirror its never-ending cycle. We cannot comprehend the magnitude of its depth. Yet we know it is there.

As life speeds up it becomes more important for us to retain our sense of marvel toward the world and heavens. Take time to ponder the sunsets and sunrises. Touch in with the greatness that we all share. Nourish your soul with the splendor of nature.

Today I will touch in with the beauty of nature and, as a result, with my own spirituality.

DAY 151

---○---

*"Often the difference between a successful man and a
failure is not one's better abilities or ideas, but
the courage that one has to bet on his ideas,
to take a calculated risk—and to act."*
MAXWELL MALTZ

Great leaders are courageous. They fight for what is right. They have the vision to see clearly the consequences of injustice and falsehoods. They not only direct others to correct wrongs, but they lead the way as well.

Take the reins of the courage you need to drive your visions through to completion. Along the way, many will fight you. They will try to dishearten you as you quest for the completion of your purpose. You must fight back. The troops you lead need the inspiration of a fearless leader who is willing to enter into a battle in the name of principles and righteousness. Do it for the cause. Then let your courage cause it to happen.

*My courageousness in the name of my principles and vision is
legendary. Through my example I inspire others to greatness.*

DAY 152

"Do all the good you can,
By all the means you can,
In all the ways you can,
In all the places you can,
At all the times you can,
To all the people you can,
As long as ever you can."

JOHN WESLEY

*D*oing good should be on the forefront of all leaders'
minds. Watch every action you take to be sure that
there is an overall benefit to humanity. Misguided leaders put
themselves and their own benefits in front of everything else. As
a result, they seldom truly succeed in achieving their visions.

The more good you do with an unselfish focus toward serving
others, the more likely you will reap the rewards for that good.
Remember that as you are honing your vision, developing goals
and plans, and carrying them forth. Your associates will work
harder for a greater cause. You will feel better about the time and
energies you dedicate to your leadership if you feel the urgency
of your contribution. Mostly, a natural law prevails that rewards
those who seek to serve others.

I approach my visions, goals, and plans
with an eye toward the greater good.

DAY 153

*"There never were in the world two opinions alike,
no more than two hairs or two grains; the
most universal quality is diversity."*
MICHEL EYQUEM DE MONTAIGNE

*P*ersuasion is an art form that has experienced great changes. In the past, leaders could persuade people to do a task just by telling them to do it. There was little argument. The leader had all the information, and the worker was there to do just that—work. No one permitted them to disagree. In exchange, workers got job security.

Now workers are better educated. Their skills are more developed. They have to be accountable. A bad decision could cost everyone involved. The most effective leaders take advantage of the diversity, both cultural and functional, within their team and encourage input from all levels. It is easy to persuade people in the right direction if they know what the direction is and feel that they have had a say in the plan. The old persuasiveness was closed and unbending. The new persuasiveness is open and flexible to the input and relies on ideas of others.

*My openness allows me to competently persuade people with logic
and reason rather than with power and force.*

DAY 154

---○---

"A horse never runs so fast as when he has other horses to catch up and outpace."

OVID

We are in a new era of hyper-competitiveness. Leaders are fundamentally rethinking the way they position themselves and their organizations. If you lead a for-profit or nonprofit organization, chances are you feel the effects. When profit-based organizations can compete effectively with not-for-profits, for example, nonprofits must thoroughly explore the way they do business or they will disappear.

Our capitalist society exists because of the exciting rivalries between organizations, all striving to provide better service at better prices. Communicate the importance of competition, and welcome its efficiency at generating results into your organization. Work with your team to identify the competition and stride boldly to outpace everyone in your class.

Competition will not go away. As long as you cooperate with it instead of fight against it, you will remain viable in these times of organizational change and turmoil.

Increased competition is inevitable. I welcome it with open arms and develop strategies to excel in the competitive arena.

DAY
155

---○---

*"The business executive is by profession a decision maker.
Uncertainty is his opponent. Overcoming
it is his mission."*

JOHN MCDONALD

*W*hat an overwhelming amount of information you
deal with on a daily basis. It seems like there is
never an end to it. Having information at your grasp to measure
probabilities from a number of outlooks is crucial to the decision-
making process. You can compare and contrast internal and external variables. Competitive information is right at your fingertips.

No matter how much information you have, the bottom line
is that eventually you need to make decisions. Other members
of your team may help evaluate the data and make recommendations, but nothing happens until you act on the information.
Do not get caught up in the Analysis Paralysis Syndrome caused
by information overload. You will never have all the details you
need. The most you can hope for is to exploit your experience
and that of your team and take the plunge. Nothing is risk free.
The only true risk is the risk of not taking any action at all.

*I capably manage the information I need to make decisions and
effectively use that information to make expeditious
decisions in all matters of importance.*

DAY 156

---○---

*"To succeed it is necessary to accept the world
as it is and rise above it."*
MICHAEL KORDA

*T*here is so much we would change to make the world a nicer place. Less crime would be a good start. The end of hunger perhaps. No children in poverty. Peace among nations and within families. No addictions. No lack of faith and feelings of despair.

At the same time we are blessed with an exceptional amount of beauty and hope to counteract the strife. Yet we still want more. If only there were more flowers. More sunny days. If only the air always had that magical smell that accompanies a summer rain. If only every love was like the first, the kind that makes every sense more alert and every nerve ending tremble.

Life is a balance. You would not know how good the good was if it were not for the suffering and anguish. You cannot change the entire world. You can make a dent. Stake out your claim, your cause. Work on it to do your part. Otherwise accept what you cannot change and revel in mysteries, tragedies, and blessings that help us to feel.

*I am able to see the balance of Earth's bounty and austerity
and work in small ways to make the world better.*

DAY 157

"*Experience is of no ethical value. It is merely the name men give to their mistakes.*"
OSCAR WILDE

*P*eople often rely heavily on experience when making decisions about other people's capabilities. Granted, having experience in a certain area is a good indicator that someone at least knows the dynamics of a situation. Experience does not mean that they have become experts, however. This is especially true in changing marketplaces and economies.

With everything changing, experience in a given situation or market does not guarantee success. It is just one of the factors that influence whether or not someone is qualified. Look for references, market knowledge, analytical abilities, training, and attitude. Take into account all competencies that make up potential new members to your team. The experience may not be a great fit. That is fine, if their attitude demonstrates a willingness to remold to fit new situations. Your job is to do the molding. Help them develop the unique competence you need to accomplish your mission.

When I evaluate the qualifications of potential new associates, I capably take into account all areas that measure their expertise and competencies.

DAY
158

---○---

*"It is wonderful how quickly you get used to things,
even the most astonishing."*

EDITH NESBIT

*W*e are amazingly adaptable animals. Many other species of life on the planet easily perish with the slightest change in their environments. Most fish can survive only the slightest change in average water temperature before they are forced to migrate or die. A four-degree change in global temperature would wipe out most of the plants in the existing rain forests.

Yet we humans keep on going. We move from climate to climate with little effect. We change our diets. We change our jobs. We change our governments. We change our minds. As we zoom into the new age of information, it is good to realize how adaptable we are. As such easily adaptable creatures, it is hard for us to relate to the needs of other life forms, and we must remember the new burdens on our resources. It is our responsibility to minimize the damage we cause as we adjust to the changes in our lives and in our environments.

*I realize the impact of many of the changes humans are forcing upon
the earth. I commit to minimizing my personal impact
on other creatures and plants.*

DAY 159

"There's only one real sin, and that is to persuade oneself that the second-best is anything but the second-best."
DORIS LESSING

What are you doing to be sure that you are the best at what you do? The dynamics of your position are changing at warp speed. The demands from your associates are ever increasing. Your customers want more and are fast to let you know that if you do not provide it, the competition will.

You need to be the very best leader. Your organization relies on you to help it be its best through these challenging times. Your associates and team members depend on you to calmly steer them through rough seas with unwavering dedication and direction. Your commitment to personal excellence motivates them to their own forms of personal excellence. Prosperity comes through being the absolute best in the eyes of your customers and partners.

I am fully energized in my pursuit of excellence. My associates and my organization are counting on me to set the tone for them to follow.

DAY 160

---○---

*"Education is a great money maker, not by
extortion, but by production."*
HORACE MANN

*A*n environment that celebrates education creates an
enlightened and skilled workforce. Development
should be an ongoing process for all people. The skills that were
essential yesterday may be totally useless today.

Leaders find ways to help their teams develop new skills even
if the organization resists. Team members themselves may not see
the value of increasing their skills. You must find a way to convince
them of the need. Focus on your vision and what that will mean
in terms of the expertise you need from others. Then help them
achieve that expertise. It will keep them productive when the
world is in flux and help you achieve your mission and goals.

*I persistently encourage a learning culture so
that we may continue to be the best.*

DAY 161

"Everything that irritates us about others can lead us to an understanding of ourselves."
CARL JUNG

*P*sychologists observe that we tend to get most irritated with others when they do things that mirror our own inadequacies. This is especially true when we are annoyed with someone but have difficulty articulating exactly what it is about the person that bothers us. It is hard to face our own inadequacies, and our subconscious makes us not even like talking about them. All we know is that we get angry and cannot explain why.

When others really bug you, ask yourself why. Honestly appraise their behaviors. What are their weaknesses? Where do you find areas where their weaknesses run parallel with yours? What are their strengths? When you assess their strengths, you may discover areas that you overlooked because of your focus on their negative points. If others' faults mirror your own, you have a responsibility to them and to yourself to focus also on their strengths.

When I become irritated with others, I honestly focus on their strengths as well as their weaknesses.

DAY 162

---○---

*A*re you as organized as you would like to be? The more organized you are, the more likely you will be to answer an emphatic no to that question. Perhaps organized people are so adamant about wanting to be more organized because they have seen the benefits of concentrating their efforts on the most important things. Focusing on what is important is the key to reaping the benefits from organization.

You can make lists all day long. You can meticulously note every event in your planner. Yet unless you develop the skill of prioritizing and focusing on the urgent, you will never be organized. Remember, too, that just focusing on the important will not make you an organized leader. You have to develop the discipline to act consistently on the important, even if it is not as easy as acting on the trivial.

*I constantly act to focus my attention and energy
on the important issues I face. I am a model of
discipline and organization as a result.*

162

DAY
163

———○———

"Take rest; a field that has rested gives a beautiful crop."
OVID

No mind can run constantly. Leaders today are under so much pressure that they seldom take a rest. They put in long hours. Even when sleeping, many leaders' dreams are filled with the crises of the day. Many are afraid to take a vacation for fear of losing control of their people or processes. They often fear losing their jobs if they are perceived as dispensable.

Do not fall into this trap. Take time out. Make sure that you take a break, even for a few hours or a few days. Clear your mind of the challenges of your position. Talk to others outside of your field in order to gain new perspectives. Read books. Relax.

If you constantly plod through the same circumstances without a break you lose sight of the rest of the world. Your perspective becomes blurry. Ironically, the more you hang on without periodic rest, the worse your performance will be. Go for excellence instead by resting your mind and body in a new setting.

Today I will take action to find a change of scenery. My mind and body need periodic breaks to keep me fresh and ready to face the challenges of my position.

DAY
164

*"It is hard to fail, but it is worse never
to have tried to succeed."*
THEODORE ROOSEVELT

As a leader you take action on many fronts in an effort to succeed. Whether it is your own personal success or your organization's success, you are the most aware of the importance of action. Many people rely on your prodding and inspiration for their own success.

Focus them on the reasons to take action. Many people you deal with will have a fear of failure. They think it is better not to act when they think there is a possibility for failure. Help them to confront their fears. Sometimes it just takes another person to show someone how irrational his or her fear is for that person to gain the motivation to take action. Help them see the potential they have for achievement. You are unique in your ability to motivate others toward growth and prosperity.

I recognize when others need my help to overcome their fears and take action toward their own successes. I confront them when necessary to encourage them to move on.

DAY
165

---○---

"Humility must always be the portion of any man who receives acclaim earned in the blood of his followers and the sacrifices of his friends."
DWIGHT D. EISENHOWER

*L*eaders should not be modest when faced with an opportunity to demonstrate their credibility. Few people have your particular ability to get the job done and lead others by virtue of your vision, strength, and courage. Be willing to brag about your accomplishments. Do not confuse modesty with humility, however. Humility involves recognizing that others have done exceptional things, and you respect them for it. Humble people show great deference in their words and their deeds.

Many people have struggled to move mountains so that your climb could be easier. They have fought battles for you. They have opened doors for you. They have stayed up late at night helping you achieve your goals. They will continue to do so because of your strength of purpose. Show them humility. Honor them with words and actions. Let them know your appreciation, and let the world know that without them you could not be where you are today.

Today I will take action to honor those who have helped me in my life. They deserve my humble recognition for their tireless efforts on my behalf.

DAY 166

---○---

*U*ltimately your success is the result of how well you
work with people. Leaders without interpersonal
skills only move others by virtue of the power of their position.
Power results from job titles or rank in the organization, but if
you convince people to act solely by using that power, you will
find that they are either weakly motivated by fear or reluctantly
motivated by practicality. If you rely on position power, you will
lose.

Develop personal power. Personal power is the power you have
when you can develop compelling visions and show others their
gains by working with you. As the educational level of people
you lead increases along with their expectations to be involved in
decision-making processes, your need for interpersonal skills will
grow exponentially. Develop greater interpersonal skills and maximize your personal power at the same time.

*Excellent interpersonal skills are essential to my leadership mastery.
I focus on developing those skills so I can motivate people
using personal power instead of position power.*

DAY 167

"I don't know the key to success, but the key to failure is trying to please everybody."

BILL COSBY

*O*ne of the negative sides of being an effective leader is that you take stands that create enemies. We all want to be liked. It can be extremely demoralizing when you think people do not like you. If you are leading along a controversial front, chances are your opposition will be extremely vocal in their denouncements of your ideas. Even if you are not controversial, some people will disagree with your vision. They will tell all who will listen.

You have to accept the fact that you will not always be popular with everyone if you are going to be visionary. Remember that when people use personal attacks to gain support against your cause, they are usually attacking your positions. If you are leading a virtuous, principled life, you do not need to defend yourself. That part will be evident. Always defend positions. Protect your positions from all fronts. Plan for differences of opinions, and develop answers for them when you are developing your plans.

I understand that by virtue of being a visionary leader my ideas will not always be popular. My vision for a common good overrides my need to be liked by everyone.

DAY
168

---○---

"Life is not a static thing. The only people who do not
change their minds are incompetents in asylums,
who can't, and those in cemeteries."
EVERETT M. DIRKSEN

*F*rom one day to the next we do not know what will
develop to take us to a new level of technology, politics,
or economics. People look to leaders to provide them with a
sense of stability. In a constantly shifting world, your vision and
firmness of purpose may be all that others have to hold on to.

You have an obligation to be sure that the vision and purpose
are flexible. If you maintain your steadfastness when all indications
are that the changing world has made your concept obsolete, you
do a great disservice to those who follow you. You have to adjust
to meet the changing times. You seldom have to give up your
vision. Constantly evaluate it. Be willing to make the small adjust-
ments to keep it current and relevant as the environment changes.

I will take steps today to evaluate my vision and purpose. My
flexibility ensures the survival of my vision and
keeps it exciting and relevant.

DAY 169

A lot of people believed that humans could never walk on the moon. A few people with vision were able to convince the world it could be done. Then they did it. People thought that the Soviet Union would never fall. Regardless, some leaders had a fervent belief and vision of a better future. They were able to tumble a monolith while others stood bellowing that it was impossible.

Perhaps the things you wish to accomplish are not as grand as space travel or international political change, but surely you are finding some disbelief and resistance for your ideas. When people have done things one way for a long time, it is hard to convince them that there is any other way. They may truly believe that you cannot accomplish your vision. Hold tight to it anyway. If you can see it, if you believe it, if you have evidence that it can be done, your leadership abilities will cause it to happen. Be resolute in your purpose and determined at every step.

*I am resolute in the pursuit of my dreams. The more people say
that what I want to do cannot be done, the more strength
I find to prove that it can be done.*

DAY 170

---○---

*"You can't push a wave onto the shore any faster
than the ocean brings it in."*
SUSAN STRASBERG

*D*id you ever have one of those days when everything seemed to go wrong? When outside forces seemed to get in the way of all your best-laid plans? You can struggle and fight and still not get that last bit of approval on a project because someone is on vacation. You feel out of control because your time lines and deadlines do not seem possible. Usually, at the last minute, everything comes together.

If you analyze what happened, you come to the conclusion that the delays were for the best for some reason or another. Leaders are controllers. You like to be in charge. You want to complete your vision on *your* time line. Your time line is not always the best. There are energies working at all times that help to determine when everything fits together logically. If you trust that they exist, you will sleep better during those stressful times when nothing seems to be going your way. It is going the way it should. Trust in the unknown force. It works for your benefit.

*Not everything is under my control. When things are not
going my way, I remember to trust in the unseen forces.*

DAY 171

---○---

*I*t is amazing how often friends and colleagues come to us with problems and are totally unaware of the causes. They want easy solutions. Many times they do not want to confront the real issues, even if we try to point them out. Instead, it seems as if they want confirmation that they have been victimized in some way or that everything will get better if they just stick with it a little longer.

It is a tremendous challenge to get others to see and accept circumstances that they prefer to ignore. In reality, most people know the situations for what they really are, but a complex set of denial mechanisms sets in. Your persistence in gently helping others to see reality can make a positive difference in their lives and in their organizations. Your understanding that they will not see reality until they are ready to can save you from much frustration.

*I understand that people will not always choose to see the obvious
for their own reasons. I persist in gently opening their
perspective when they are ready.*

DAY 172

---○---

"To follow, without halt, one aim:
There's the secret of success."
ANNA PAVLOVA

*T*he world is full of choices. They are all attainable. They all have value. Success comes from evaluating all the options available, then finally making a choice. This is where many people experience downfalls. They cannot decide among all the wonderful opportunities that are always present. They decide either to attempt to try all the opportunities they see or never to apply themselves to any. Either choice is painful because of the unreached potential.

Make a choice. Decide your one purpose. Pursue it with all your heart. You will achieve success in greater measures than you ever anticipated.

If you already have chosen, now is a good time to evaluate whether you are sticking to your one purpose. Are you maintaining your course without fail? Remember, your purpose must remain singular and constant. Your plans for how to get there can change, depending on circumstances and opportunities.

Today I take action to review my purpose and ensure that
I am acting constantly on it with a singular focus.

DAY 173

"All great changes are irksome to the human mind, especially those which are attended with great dangers and uncertain effects."
JOHN ADAMS

As a leader you are probably willing to grasp the reins of change and ride it wherever it takes you. Your particular ability to adapt has propelled you into the position you have now. Whether you are a person who reluctantly adapts to change with an eye toward reality or a person who embraces change as the ultimate opportunity, dealing with people who resist change will be difficult.

Many of your associates are fighting the changes they face, especially when they are accompanied by a decline in personal or professional security. If you want others to embrace change, see it through their eyes. What does it mean for them? What do they think they will lose as a result? What are the benefits of the change that might make them more accepting? Be supportive and understanding. Encourage them by helping them diminish their losses and see the opportunities.

I understand that my ability to deal effectively with change is not a common trait, and I do all I can to help others see the opportunities of change and diminish the threat.

DAY 174

---○---

*"He that can please nobody is not so much
to be pitied as he that nobody can please."*
CALEB COLTON

When you have a vision, it is difficult to be patient and kind to those whom you feel are not doing their part to bring it to fruition. It is so clear in your mind. It seems so easy. It is difficult to understand why some people just cannot get it through their heads. Why don't they get it?

When you begin to feel this way, you will no doubt be more critical than you need to be. People respond more immediately to positive reinforcement than to negative reinforcement. You get results by looking for the areas where they are on board with your vision and rewarding that behavior. You set an example by giving the attention to the team members who are performing to your expectations. Your other team members want your approval. They want to be on board. Be patient. Win them over with praise.

*I make it a priority to find positive behaviors to praise in
all of my associates. I am able to motivate others by
energetically focusing on what they do right.*

DAY 175

---○---

*"The highest service we can perform for others is
to help them help themselves."*

HORACE MANN

You are probably exceptionally skilled in your area of expertise. You can do much of the work needed faster and better than most people. That is how you got where you are. You were, and continue to be, able to impress others with your competence. It most likely gives you a great deal of satisfaction to perform so masterfully.

Because you are so skilled and have always been rewarded for your mastery, you will be tempted into the trap of doing parts of your job that others should be learning. If you are to advance, then you owe it to yourself to be sure that you have qualified people prepared in your area of expertise. You have to take the time to help them and teach them. They deserve the opportunity to learn. You deserve the opportunity to grow.

*Today I will look at those areas where I should be moving on
and take action to develop others to replace my expertise.*

DAY 176

---

*"Good government obtains when those who are near are
made happy, and those who are far off are attracted."*
CONFUCIUS

*T*here has been a lot of discussion about the use of
benchmarking as a technique to find the best and
highest level of operational practice within an organization. It
means that you find someone who does what you do exceptionally well and copy what he or she is doing.

By benchmarking, you may make your end customers happier.
They may buy from you out of convenience or out of true satisfaction. If you are personally benchmarking a truly effective leader,
you will find that those you lead are happier. The danger of
benchmarking is that it can take away from innovation. In a
changing world, if you just copy what others are doing, by the
time you implement your programs they have probably changed
their own. You stay one step behind.

Be the kind of organization or leader that others benchmark.
Do the things you need to do in such an exciting way that others
cannot resist copying you. Benchmark others, but be sure that
others are also benchmarking you.

*I work to learn what I can from others. I realize that I also need
to innovate and develop new systems and ideas. I am making
my mark when others are benchmarking from me.*

DAY 177

---○---

*"The man with the average mentality, but with control,
with a definite goal, and a clear conception of how
it can be gained, and above all, with the power
of application and labor, wins in the end."*
WILLIAM HOWARD TAFT

*T*he world is overflowing with geniuses who never reach their full potential. Sometimes extreme intelligence or academic credentials can do more harm than good in building a prosperous leadership style. Unless careful, the gifted academic may choose to analyze too much, to look at things from too many sides, and to avoid making decisions for the lack of sufficient data.

Your level of education and your ability to score well on standardized testing are not great indicators of your ability to lead. Your decisiveness, purpose, and passionate direction will do more for you than any university honor. Your vision and the ability to communicate that vision to others will get you more followers than a test score. Remember that IQ is secondary to your passion, purpose, vision, and direction. Without them, you are like a computer with nothing to compute.

*I continually take steps to assure a singularity of purpose. My
passionate ability to communicate my vision and goals
is more important than any other measure.*

DAY 178

---○---

*"The distribution of talents in this world should
not be our concern. Our responsibility is to take
the talents we have and ardently parlay them
to the highest possible achievement."*

ALAN LOY MCGINNIS

What are your talents? Are you using them to your fullest potential? Often leaders think that they have to do everything well. Leaders should have a working knowledge of their area, but it is impossible to know everything. Equally, there is no way you can be talented in everything.

Strive mostly for self-knowledge. Understand your natural abilities. Remember that to have a talent does not mean that you have to be the best at it. Even natural abilities need development and refinement. If something comes naturally to you, you like doing it, and others notice it, chances are it is a talent. Exploit it. Round out your abilities by finding others with complementary talents. This way you can develop a team that can accomplish anything.

*Today I will assess my talents and determine how best to use
them to reach my vision. I find and develop others with
complementary talents to round out the team.*

DAY 179

---○---

*"Reason can answer questions, but imagination
has to ask them."*

ALEX F. OSBORN

*D*oing crazy things can help stimulate your creativity. Are you being crazy enough? Unfortunately, most people spend too much time in the same old place every day doing the same old thing. It is hard for your imagination to soar beyond the four walls of your office if you are always there.

Before you can come up with new ideas, plans, and objectives you need to ask yourself many questions about your direction. You need to ask if opportunities will work in your environment. You cannot even see these opportunities from the same old perch. Leave. Walk in the park. Go on retreat. Ride a merry-go-round. Feed the dolphins at a theme park. March in a parade. Do things that are outside of your norm, and you will find a multitude of new and exciting questions and opportunities bouncing around in your head.

Craziness helps stimulate creativity. Today I will do something completely out of the ordinary so that I can get out of my regular environment and expand my opportunities.

DAY 180

*E*very day we do things by habit. Most people get up at the same time, drink coffee from the same cup, put their clothes on in the exact same sequence, and take the exact same route to work.

Habits are good. If we had to think every action through before we moved on it, we would never act. Excellence can be a habit. Repeat quality behaviors over and over again, and they will eventually become habits. You do them without even thinking. It takes a while to develop any habit. You must be conscious of the activity until it becomes routine. Once that happens, you only have to use caution to avoid replacing the good habit with a bad one. Cultivate excellence as a habit. Consciously take steps to be only the best. Replace bad habits with habits of excellence, and you will excel in all areas of your life.

I cultivate excellence as a habit. Doing and being my best propels me in my life and my aspirations.

DAY 181

──────◯──────

*"Hold fast to dreams for if dreams die, life is
a broken-winged bird that cannot fly."*
LANGSTON HUGHES

When you are a visionary, there are plenty of people who will stand in the way of the accomplishment of your dreams. There are hundreds of reasons why what you dream cannot happen. There are thousands of obstacles in your way. Some people will attempt to discourage you out of petty jealousy—they cannot stand to see anyone get ahead of them. Other people will try to discourage you out of what they perceive as your best interests—they do not want to see you broken-hearted.

Only you know the value of your dreams. Only you know the potential of your vision on your life and the lives of others. You are the motivating force behind your dreams. You make them happen. Do not let other people stop you. They have the power to do so only if you give it to them. Never release that power. Use it to keep your dreams alive and energized. Believe in them, and they are real.

*I hold fast to my dreams with all the power I can summon.
I have the control and the belief to make anything
I dream become a reality.*

DAY
182

*T*ime is the most valuable currency we have at our
disposal. It is more valuable than any quantity of
cash, stocks, or bonds. You can always earn more money. You
can never earn more time. Once you spend some of your time,
it is gone forever, never to be recovered.

Although you cannot earn more time than you have, you are
able to maximize its use. Make time count. Use it to enhance
your life and further your vision. Never, never waste it. If you
are wasting your time, you are throwing life's currency to the
wind. You would not do that with cash; why would you do it
with your time? Have a purpose for all of your activities. Control
your time, and you will always have enough of it to do all the
things you want to do.

*Time is my most valuable commodity. I take full responsibility
to make sure I maximize my use of it to enhance
my life and further my vision.*

DAY
183

―――○―――

*"When man has love he is no longer at the mercy
of forces greater than himself, for he, himself,
becomes the powerful force."*
LEO BUSCAGLIA

Not enough credit is given to the power of love. Love is the powerful force that helps you overcome any obstacle. Without love, life is meaningless. We are not just talking about romantic love here. We are talking about pure, true, unconditional love for yourself and for others.

Leaders love life. They love challenges. They love their purpose. They love themselves. Through your love of yourself you gain the confidence you need to accomplish your goals and implement your vision. Mostly, however, leaders love others. Through your unconditional love of others you help them grow and mature.

When you love others, your purpose takes on a greater meaning. Let love into your leadership. Let it be unconditional. It will return more to you than ever you could have hoped.

*I openly love myself and others, realizing the powerful force
of unconditional love. Through my willingness
to love, great things happen.*

DAY
184

---○---

"Always leave enough time in your life to do something that makes you happy, satisfied, or even joyous. That has more of an effect on economic well-being than any other single factor."

PAUL HAWKEN

*C*hances are that you dedicate an inordinate amount of time and energy to tasks related to your purpose. Even if you are not there physically, you are probably there mentally. There is nothing wrong with this as it is your purposeful approach that assures your success. Still, you will find that taking a break now and then will help you regroup your thoughts and recharge your energies for the tasks you need to complete.

When was the last time you did something that really gave you a joyous feeling? Spend time with your family. Help a youngster learn to throw a ball and revel in the excitement when his or her little hands master the coordination you taught. Go to a movie. Take an art class and decorate a canvas or piece of clay with your own brand of beauty. You need the mental break. Take it and watch what happens when you return to your vision.

Today I will schedule time to do something different that brings beauty and joy to my life.

DAY 185

---○---

"Not failure, but low aim, is a crime."
JAMES RUSSELL LOWELL

*T*here are times in all persons' lives when they just feel the need to sit back and coast for a while. It seems nice to enjoy a rest when things start to become easier after a long struggle. Resting is great, but if it goes on too long, then perhaps the problem is more associated with not aiming high enough on all levels.

If you find tremendous financial success, for example, and then retire to play golf, what purpose has your life had? Look at the world around you. What could you be doing to make it a better place? Do not accept it for what it is. You have talent and abilities that no one else has. When you reach your highest aims in one area, focus that energy and passion on another. Life is most rewarding when you aim high in all areas of life.

As I experience success in some areas of my life, I continually evaluate other spheres where I can dedicate my passion and talents to enhance my life and that of others.

DAY 186

No one is born into greatness. Scientists will never discover a greatness gene. People may be born into privilege and opportunity, but that is meaningless. History has demonstrated repeatedly that the privileged ranks are just as rife with failures and unfulfilled lives as any other. One of the great beauties of the world we live in is that anyone can be great.

Greatness is a mind-set. Determination to change a wrong into a right builds greatness. A passionate dream to make a contribution to the lives of others who are less fortunate establishes greatness. A belief that you can make a better life for yourself and your family, combined with action, sends you soaring toward greatness. Greatness comes wrapped in passion, in dreams, and in the unabashed willingness to do anything that needs to be done to reach your vision.

*My confident and passionate desire to achieve my dreams is the first
step to personal greatness. The action I take daily to reach
my dreams secures my majesty.*

DAY 187

> *"A professional is one who does his best work*
> *when he feels the least like working."*
> FRANK LLOYD WRIGHT

*A*ll leaders have days when they wake up and ask themselves if it is all worth it. Sometimes the answer comes back negative. Other times they just cannot be sure. They still get up, get dressed, and fulfill their obligations. There are too many people relying on them. They have set a behemoth into motion. Even under terrible stress and personal uncertainty they have to continue moving.

When this feeling happens to you, look to the future. Remind yourself of the ultimate purpose for all your labor. When the dream is fuzzy, recall it and clarify it. Paint it again across your mind's eye in vivid colors. You will gain the energy and the enthusiasm. Remember that when you are feeling at your lowest, the tide is about to turn. The stressful times eventually pass. Rather than being dragged out to sea in a tempest, you will soon be gently lifted back onto the sunny shore.

Today I will work to make my vision even clearer and more vivid.
This helps me build the strength I need to continue moving
toward it even during difficult times.

DAY 188

---

*"The trick is to make sure you don't die
waiting for prosperity to come."*

LEE IACOCCA

There are no guarantees in life. You cannot be sure you or those you love will be alive tomorrow. We all know that, yet it is amazing how many people live only for the future, sacrificing some of the most important things they have today. Celebrate your relationships now. Make those you are around feel important.

Take your family on a vacation. Sure, if you wait just a few more years you will be able to afford something better. The kids might not want to go then. Choose something less luxurious. Add laughter and fond memories to your life for the years to come. If you always wanted to paint, do it today. You never know what tomorrow will bring. There is always a need for sacrifice. You cannot have everything you want today. You can find substitutes and live your life today, knowing that tomorrow's uncertainties are at play.

*I take care to live my life for today while balancing future needs
and desires. Today I will tell someone how important she
or he is to me and make plans to demonstrate it.*

DAY 189

---○---

*"Frankness is the backbone of friendship—when
it is covered by the flesh of tact."*

G. G. COLMORE

We are lucky in life to have a few good friends. The more successful you become, the harder it is to find friends who love you for who you are rather than what you are. Anyone in a high position would have difficulty denying that fact. Welcome friends into your life who are not afraid to tell you the things you most need to hear. Too often we like to have friends who agree with us on all issues, yet what do we learn from them?

In the same fashion, be a counselor to your friends. Do so only when asked, then be forthcoming with opinions and feelings that will help them be better people. Some truths are just too painful to hear. The truth can only help if it is wrapped cautiously in the padding that only a knowing, loving friend could find. Be careful with your friends. They are too precious to lose because of mismanaged intentions. At the same time they are too precious to allow to hurt themselves, when you can help them stop.

*I am a good friend and am forthcoming whenever I am asked
to be. At the same time I welcome frankness from
the friends I love and respect.*

DAY 190

"Life shrinks or expands in proportion to one's courage."
ANAÏS NIN

We tend to associate the word *courage* most often with war. Bravery in battle is honored and respected across cultures. Is your role as a leader much different from that of a general during wartime? People's lives and livelihoods are at stake with every decision you make. Your own security is in jeopardy whenever you take a stand. Your organization could fall to the competition if you do not act with bravery and strategy.

The competitive nature of society and the business world forces you to be courageous if you are to survive. Those you lead base their actions on their perceptions of your courage. Never be afraid to hold the line on your ideals. If you are right, you are meant to win. The battle is being fought on all fronts. Your courageous manner is the ammunition that holds your team together and helps them to win.

I am a courageous leader and take steps today to do what is necessary to help my team and organization win, regardless of the personal danger I face.

DAY 191

---○---

*T*here is a tremendous amount of suffering in the world. Homelessness is epidemic. The breakdown of the family is contributing to a decline in overall morality and poverty. Drug use is destroying bright young minds. Killing is occurring on a daily basis around the globe.

You may feel compelled to climb into a cocoon and ignore the problems and strife surrounding you. After all, you are working hard. Your values are intact. You are building and growing. Never lose touch with your spirituality and the compassion that is a primary component of it. Look at world problems with an eye toward helping. Your abilities can contribute to helping make the world safer, more peaceful, and loving. You have a responsibility to give back. Feel with your soul. You are connected with those who are suffering. Find ways to help them. Your touch will make a difference.

*My compassion and understanding for the challenges
others face motivate me to ease their pain.*

DAY
192

---

*"The wave of the future is coming and
there is no stopping it."*
ANNE MORROW LINDBERGH

Some people will dedicate an incredible amount of energy to fighting change. They fight process reengineering. They fight technological advances. They fight the need to learn new skills to keep fresh in a shifting marketplace. People fight change that may lead to the elimination of their livelihood.

Change cannot be stopped. Reengineering is going to continue as long as new technologies allow business to become more speedy and efficient. Leaders must persuade people that their security lies in welcoming change. Those who see it coming and find ways to work with it are the ones who will have the competitive advantage in the marketplace.

Show your associates how they can gain by embracing new ways of doing business. Help them to understand the consequences of fighting change. They cannot stop it. Persuade them instead to welcome it for all the opportunities it brings.

*It is natural for people to resist change when they feel insecure.
I continually act to demonstrate the benefits of flowing
with the force of change that cannot be stopped.*

DAY 193

*"Striving for excellence motivates you; striving
for perfection is demoralizing."*

HARRIET BRAIKER

*G*reat leaders strive for excellence in all they do. They
and their organizations are known for quality. The
word *excellence* comes from the root *excel*, which means "to be
comparatively better." It does not mean "to be perfect." If you
are confusing excellence with perfection, you will never reach
either.

If, instead of excellence, you strive for perfection, seldom will
anything be satisfactory enough for you to decide it is complete.
Absolutely nothing is perfect. If you insist on perfection at every
turn, you will be frustrated and disappointed with all you pro-
duce.

Be excellent instead of perfect. Be better than the competition.
Constantly aim for improvement. At the same time, accept your
humanity and the limitations of time, money, and ability. Do
the best you can with the resources you have. Your reputation
for excellence will propel your success.

***I avoid the frustration and disappointment of trying to be perfect. I
strive continually for excellence and the highest quality possible.***

DAY
194

———○———

*"I must admit that I personally measure success in terms
of the contributions an individual makes to her
or his fellow human beings."*
MARGARET MEAD

*T*eam management and team culture are quickly replacing traditional styles of top-down management. What does it mean to be a team? Most teams are reading team books, hiring consultants and facilitators, and learning their own brand of what teaming is.

Do not displace the individual in your zeal to seek group synergy. Teams work when everyone uses their talents to contribute to the success of the group. When the individuals are forced to subjugate their wills and opinions to the will of a majority, they will no longer provide a unique contribution. You lose what you were hoping to attain: a sense of combining all the talents, expertise, and abilities to create unique solutions and collaboration. Celebrate the individual as part of your team effort. Know everyone's strengths and how they can work to advance the team's success.

*Team synergy starts with the acknowledgment of the strengths
and talents of each member. I promote and reward
individual contributions to team success.*

DAY 195

"The past always looks better than it was;
it's only pleasant because it isn't here."
FINLEY PETER DUNNE

*P*eople often wax nostalgic about the past. Things were simple. The rules were uncomplicated. In organizations, stability reigned. Wasn't it grand?

The stability was actually an illusion based on economics. There was not much competition, and technology was static. Companies could afford to perpetuate the fantasy of security. At the same time, few minorities or women had opportunities. The company controlled life. A whole generation of fathers never got to know their children. In the end, it became evident that employee loyalty was seldom reciprocated. Few people would discard the level of physical comfort we have now. Few would bow to the needs of their organization over the needs of their families. The old days may be rosy when looking backward, but looking forward, today's opportunities, open to all members of society, are much more resplendent.

When I am tempted to look back and think things were better then,
I remember all the opportunities that exist now. Today I will
make note of all the new possibilities this time brings to me.

DAY
196

---

*"Help thy brother's boat across, and lo!
thine own has reached the shore."*
HINDU PROVERB

You will find that the most effective way of working on your own success is to work on the success of others. You can have a profound impact on the advancement of the people in your life. Many people need your support to grow. What have you done recently to help your boss accomplish his or her aspirations? What about people who work with or for you? What have you done for your family and friends? What about your spiritual family? Your neighbors? Your professional network?

Find out from other people what their dreams are. Ask questions. Show a real interest in what they want to accomplish. Helping them does not have to take a lot of time. Sometimes all someone needs is an encouraging word so that he or she can rustle up the nerve to take action on his or her own vision. Every step that you take to help someone else brings you one step closer to the fulfillment of your own dreams.

*I am a supportive friend, colleague, and family member. I encourage
others to reach their own pinnacle, and magically
I reach mine in the process.*

DAY 197

"Idealists . . . foolish enough to throw caution to the winds, have advanced mankind and have enriched the world."

EMMA GOLDMAN

*I*dealism is often the mark of youth and inexperience. With maturity comes the realization that the world is not a perfect place, and anything that will move it toward perfection will take too much energy. Cynicism can be comforting, because it lets you off the hook. Cynics never have to invest the energy to right a wrong. They can insist nothing can be done anyway.

Do not let the hopeful attitude of your youth be replaced by cynicism. Doubt and pessimism will do nothing for you. Your beliefs about the world at large spill over into your beliefs about your own success. Be idealistic. The world may never be perfect. Still, like the process of continual improvement in an organization, small changes at regular intervals will have a positive effect on all the world's ills. You make a difference by maintaining a certain idealistic innocence and optimism and carrying it through in your leadership style.

I work to maintain a degree of hopeful idealism in all my activities. It keeps me young and helps me make a positive contribution to the world.

DAY 198

"Understanding comes through communications, and
through understanding we find the way to peace."
RALPH SMEDLEY

*I*t is ironic that with all the advances in communications technologies people are complaining more than ever about the lack of communication. Even though people are transmitting and receiving information at a higher rate and faster speed than ever before, they are conversing less about what that information means to them.

True communication occurs when people take part in dialogue. They openly, honestly, and actively give and take. They listen to each other and learn from each other. They confront without fear. They speak to a human and expect a human response, with all the vocal inflection, facial expression, and eye contact to say what the words themselves cannot communicate. Encourage more real communication with the people in your life. Information transfer technology is not communication. It can never replace human contact.

I continually endeavor to make wise use of information technology
and not let it replace real communication. This approach keeps
me constantly aware of the needs of the people in my life.

DAY 199

---◯---

*"Do I not destroy my enemies when
I make them my friends?"*
ABRAHAM LINCOLN

Politics will always play a big part in your growth and in the accomplishment of your visions. You need to continually make realistic appraisals of who people are aligned with and what their interests are. Because you have passionate interests and dreams, you will find that people with opposing interests will fight you. They will try to sabotage you and stop you from attaining your goals if they are contrary to their own.

Most people in this situation feel an urge to draw a line in the sand. If someone is going to oppose you, then it is war. War means fighting battles. War means having enemies and trying to vanquish them by any means possible. It does not have to be that way. You can find commonality with those who oppose you. A realistic view of where compromise and connection can be made goes a long way toward having people who might be your enemies help you achieve your passion.

*My own goals and interests often run contrary to
the goals and interests of others. Today I will take
steps toward compromise and connection with
someone who might otherwise be my enemy.*

DAY 200

"Ideas won't keep. Something must be done about them."
ALFRED NORTH WHITEHEAD

As organizations become team oriented, they are finding that more and more of people's time is taken up with meetings. People complain that the quantity of meetings they have to attend is exorbitant. When meetings do not accomplish objectives, when the participation is one-sided, or when nothing is done with the ideas and information shared, many will rightly feel that they have wasted their time.

Whether you are running business, civic, or family meetings, always be sure that a plan of action comes out of them. There is nothing more debilitating to the energy a group generates around an idea than not to act on it. It is a waste of time and money to bring people together to be creative, to talk about situations and ideas, and then have them leave with no closure. Develop action plans. Ask people to take responsibility for different parts of it. Follow up to be sure it is being completed. Then in your next meeting, brag about the group's progress and celebrate their success.

I have the ability to competently and confidently guide people in creative and productive meetings. I make sure that action is always taken on all new ideas and goals.

DAY 201

"You have to expect to win, because
if you don't you already have lost."
RICKY HUNLEY

*C*onfidence guarantees your success. You never see a boxer win a fight without first announcing to the world how great he is. If you enter any situation thinking that you might lose, your competitors will sense a lack of confidence, and they will take full advantage of it. The people you lead will feel a lack of confidence and never commit fully.

Be confident in your vision. Picture success in your mind. Know that wherever you are going, whatever your plans, you will find the way. Do not fear failure, or it will be the conqueror. Do not fear success. If you do, your fear will work on your subconscious and prevent you from taking the actions you need to achieve it. Believe wholeheartedly in your abilities and the abilities of your team. Your skills and abilities may be the physical manifestation that brings you to success. Your confidence is the spiritual manifestation that guarantees it.

I am in control of the skills and abilities that I need to create success.
My confidence is the magic I possess that guarantees it.

DAY 202

---○---

"One should not search for an abstract meaning of life.
Everyone has his own specific vocation or mission
in life to carry out a concrete assignment
which demands fulfillment."
VIKTOR FRANKL

*M*any people tell you their purpose in life is to be successful or to be happy or to love more. These are great concepts, but they lack specificity. No one can achieve success unless they have a clear definition of what success is. No one will be happy unless they closely examine what they are doing when they are happy, then do it. No one will experience love as their life's purpose unless they themselves love through their actions, words, and deeds.

Everyone has a vocation. When you discover what it is that truly brings fulfillment, dedicate your life to it. You will never feel true success unless you are doing what you feel most compelled to do. Never deny your purpose so that you may fulfill someone else's. Fulfill your own, and success will walk by your side wherever you choose to go.

I continually strive to define my purpose in concrete and specific
terms. Success, happiness, and love are my companions
on the journey to where I feel called.

DAY
203

---○---

*"To be sincere with ourselves is better and harder than
to be painstakingly accurate with others."*
AGNES REPPLIER

*B*efore you criticize others, take a look at yourself. Take
responsibility for your own actions and their results.
In many ways our culture has become one that accepts blame
over personal responsibility. People sue other people for outland-
ish reasons. The news media is full of stories of people who find
excuses for their own actions and then look for someone else to
pay for their irresponsibility.

As a leader you can set a positive example by taking responsibility for your own actions. Let others know that when there is
blame to place you are the first to accept your part. The people
you lead are much more likely to accept accountability for their
actions when they see that you ardently accept it for yourself.

*I accept full responsibility for my own actions. My commitment
to personal accountability spurs others to readily accept
accountability for their own actions.*

DAY 204

"There cherries grow, that none can buy
Till cherry ripe themselves do cry."
RICHARD ALISON

Just as you cannot rush the maturing fruit on a tree, you also cannot rush your success as it matures and ripens. Look at what happens when tomatoes are picked green then gassed before being put on your grocery store shelf. They have the color and appearance of tomatoes, but the taste is flat and unappetizing.

Your visions work on the same principle. You may be able to rush certain aspects of your goals. Impatience may force the appearance of readiness. You will find, though, that you cannot force natural laws. Some things take more time than your patience allows, and there is nothing you can do about it. Too many variables outside your control come into play. If you rush them, your visions and goals will have the same bitter taste, the same impenetrable texture as an unripe fruit.

I resist my temptation to rush the completion of my visions and goals until all the elements fall into place. That way, I can savor them as the sweetness of fully ripened fruit.

DAY
205

*"Give us clear vision that we may know where to stand
and what to stand for—because unless we stand
for something, we shall fall for anything."*
PETER MARSHALL

You have the gift of vision. You clearly see a future that others cannot even dream. Your created image of vivid hues and colors is enchanting. Alas, it only exists in *your* mind.

For the vision to be effective, it has to exist in the minds of other people too. As with a painting, the eye is attracted to the brightest spot. Describe your vision with brilliance and clarity. Make it exciting. Make it shine. Make what is on the canvas of your mind as irresistible as a Monet.

If you communicate the energy that brings your vision alive and gives it depth, people will be attracted to it above all others. If you keep your viewpoint to yourself, they will naturally go in search of another visionary to draw another picture of what life can be like. Compel them with your vision, and they will look no further.

*Today I will take steps to make my vision bold, colorful, and exciting
in my own mind's eye. My ability to communicate to others
excites and involves them in its fulfillment.*

DAY 206

---○---

"Great deeds are usually wrought at great risks."
HERODOTUS

When the Vikings sailed across the oceans in search of new lands, their journeys were fraught with greater risk than we can imagine. Their bravery was exceptional. They navigated into uncharted waters, not even knowing if the earth was round or flat. They took the risks necessary to reap the great bounties they hoped awaited their arrival.

They were adventurers and discoverers. They were conquerors. The risk, they believed, was more exciting than the comfort and security of staying close to shore. Leadership is like that. It is an adventure. You have the opportunity to uncover new vistas.

With courage and a taste for the rewards that lie out of sight, you can journey to new continents. Your enthusiasm and sense of adventure will encourage others to risk losing sight of the shore in order to savor the abundance you know waits just over the horizon.

I am willing to take the risks necessary to reap the rewards that await me. My sense of adventure and excitement motivates others to join me on my journey.

DAY 207

---○---

"Prefer a loss to a dishonest gain: the one brings pain
at the moment, the other for all time."

CHILON

*I*t is tempting at times to bend the truth a little to meet your needs. Doing so, it seems, will hasten your gains. Who will know anyway? The moral dilemma associated with dishonesty, no matter how slight, has one unequivocal answer. Integrity.

The one thing you can never risk is your integrity. Once you lose integrity, it never comes back.

Inevitably, accomplishments derived from deceit are short-term. People who are burned eventually find out, and their memories last for the long term. Leaders who allow any level of duplicity within their organization or within their team assuredly become victims of duplicity.

Never allow the temptation for short-term gains to take away your hard-won reputation. Your vigilance over the ethics of your team and organization assures their virtue too.

My constant vigil to assure that my ethical lead is followed
assures our reputation and long-term growth.

DAY
208

---○---

*"Whenever an individual or a business decides that
success has been attained, progress stops."*
THOMAS J. WATSON

*S*uccess is not a destination. You do not arrive at success.
Success, instead, is a process. It is a journey that continues as you do things that help you reach your goals and visions. If you see success as one certain accomplishment, a certain dollar figure, or a certain acquisition, you are destined to be disappointed.

Never sit back on your haunches, thinking you are successful. Such inaction is exactly what competitors are looking for. When they see you rest, cocky and assured that you have reached the top, they swoop in and steal victory from your grasp as fast as an eagle catches its prey. Remember that success is what you are doing to reach your goals, and you will always have something to aim for.

*If I am making progress toward my vision, I am experiencing
success. As I complete old goals, I continually make
new ones to keep me on my journey.*

DAY 209

―――――○―――――

*W*hat harm could listening to reason do? It could discourage you from going ahead with plans. It could convince you that your direction is all wrong. Reason looks at the current situation and desired situation and applies logic to them. You may have plans or ideas that are not logical. Reason will highlight them.

If you are resolute in your vision and believe in all its possibilities, reason alone will not persuade you to take a different direction from the one you have chosen. It provides facts and points to areas of danger. When your belief is high, the facts will not overwhelm your intuition about what is right. Then, reason is just another tool to help you decide the direction to take with your vision and what to watch for as you proceed.

*I am resolute in my determination to succeed in the
achievement of my vision. I openly encourage
logical input from people with expertise.*

DAY 210

"It is the ability to choose that makes us human."
MADELEINE L'ENGLE

We are blessed to be living at a time in history when choice is abundant in almost all areas of life. Telephones used to come in black. That was it. Then our options expanded to five or six colors. Eventually there were five or six manufacturers. Now we decide on wireless or nonwireless, picture or voice, who will carry the signal, and a multitude of options never dreamed possible in the days of black rotary telephones.

These choices are mirrored in all aspects of our lives. You can choose your lifestyle. You can choose your career. You can choose anything. With so much choice, people become bewildered and paralyzed. They allow the current of daily life to carry them indiscriminately.

You have an incredible power to choose, one that has expanded from centuries ago. Choose your place. Make your mark. Decide what and who you are, now and for the future. It is the greatest gift change has given us. Perhaps it is also the most challenging.

I take action and make choices rather than allowing confusion to paralyze my acceptance of the gift of choice.

DAY 211

———○———

*"Most power is illusionary and perceptual. You have
to create an environment in which people
perceive you as having some power."*
CARRIE SAXON PERRY

No one can give you power. Titles are insignificant. Positions mean nothing. Plenty of people in high positions have no power.

Grasp power with your attitude and actions. Be effective and knowledgeable. As you experience success, expand your circle of influence, and build liaisons that put you on the same level as people with authority.

Your countenance is also important. Be confident and look confident. Never underestimate the importance of good posture, an assured walk, and firm speech. People use these cues to form their perceptions as much as they use positional cues. Power is little more than a perception. Create and control people's perceptions of you, and they will give you the power you need in return.

*My appearance, posture, and confidence build the power
base that will allow me to reach my goals.*

DAY 212

"It is a great deed to leave nothing for tomorrow."
BALTASAR GRACIÁN

*F*ew things are as important as identifying what is important and doing it promptly. It is tempting to work on things of little consequence, because they are easy to do. Doing them creates the illusion that you are getting things done. At least you are creating a lot of activity. For most leaders, there is so much to be done that it is hard to prioritize.

Assign importance levels to everything that comes your way. If it is a high priority, get it done. Be sure you finish everything that is high priority before it becomes a emergency. Handling emergencies is exciting at the time, but they rob your time and only serve to create other emergencies.

Make lists. Put things on your list that you can complete on the day you assign. If it is not urgent that it be done on the day it is assigned, it should not be on your list. Your abilities in this area will build the credibility you need to stretch your leadership authority.

I increase my effectiveness by capably prioritizing tasks and finishing them on schedule. This gives me credibility and allows me to stretch my leadership authority.

DAY 213

---

*"My own view of history is that human beings do have
genuine freedom to make choices. Our destiny is not
predetermined for us; we determine it for ourselves."*
ARNOLD TOYNBEE

*M*any people look at their personal history and blame
it for the restrictions placed upon their lives. They
may think their education will not allow them to reach a certain
level. They may feel they did not receive the adequate psychological nurturing necessary to achieve greatness. It may appear that
choices made early in life restrict the opportunities available later.

Nothing is stopping you from choosing to do or be anything
you want. Looking at people who have risen to great heights
will demonstrate that ambition and confident persistence are the
primary vehicles of success. Determine what and where you want
to be. Then tenaciously pursue the vision, checking at all angles
to find your road.

Never blame anyone other than yourself for low aspirations.
Raise them high. You are destined for greatness.

*I am destined to achieve anything I choose. Today I will examine
my limiting beliefs and discard them for a more confident
belief in my aspirations and abilities.*

DAY 214

---○---

*S*urely you would like to have everyone on the team working competently and enthusiastically toward the accomplishment of a grand vision. Some people, however, fight your vision because of their own personal alliances or agendas. Some have not developed the skills necessary to be effective. You may need certain talents that some people just do not have.

Not everyone can stay on the team. Work to be sure that everyone has all the opportunities for development you can provide. After that, it is their responsibility to decide what to do with the opportunities. If the talent is not there, or if they refuse to learn new skills, they have to go. If they fight you at every step because of malice or their own self-interests, you owe them nothing but your best wishes in their new ventures.

In our high-speed, competitive environment you need everyone skillfully and ardently working in the same direction. Hesitate only to be sure that you personally have done all you can to develop someone before ending the relationship.

Today I will work to develop people's skills so that they may stay on the team, but I am aware that not everyone is able to competently and enthusiastically help achieve the vision.

DAY 215

"When work is soulless, life stifles and dies."
ALBERT CAMUS

Work for work's sake soon becomes boring. Work for profit's sake may satisfy the direct recipient of the profit, but will do nothing for those whose only job is to help create the profit. Work should be done on a deeper level. It should reach into the soul of everyone involved in the accomplishment of your goals and deeds. Finding the soul of your group and your organization involves looking at the deeper meaning behind why the work is being done.

Where can you give back? What can you do to make the world a better place? Answer these questions, and you will find an excitement like no other.

Encourage the members of your team to define your organization's soul. Give back to the community. Help others who need your help. Become sincerely involved, and profits will result. Productivity will be a given. Good will carry your leadership and your organization to levels that self-interest and apathy could never sustain.

My purpose and the purpose of my organization go deep into the soul. I consistently search for ways my leadership can inspire benevolence and caring about the community.

DAY 216

When was the last time you felt joy? That Gene Kelly kind of singing-and-dancing-while-swinging-from-the-lamppost kind of joy. Chances are that you are not feeling like that as much as you would like. You are probably so dedicated to the development and achievement of your vision that pleasure is postponed more than it should be.

You never know what life is going to bring you, good and bad. Find ways to do things that kindle a sense of delight and rapture. Surround yourself with others who are having fun. Do something out of the ordinary. Stand on a table and recite a Shakespeare sonnet. Sing along with your car radio at the top of your lungs, and wink at the people who stare at you. Take your child or a disadvantaged child to the zoo, and imitate the monkeys.

Reawaken your sense of fun and enchantment. You will find a secondary benefit is the reawakening of the creativity you need as a leader in today's challenging environment.

*Today I will reawaken my sense of spontaneity and fun.
I will rediscover the joy that makes me
laugh and sing and energizes me.*

DAY 217

*F*ocusing on what we do not have is natural. We see a talented pianist and think of how lovely it would be to be able to play so beautifully. We see a talented ball player and wonder at the moves, wishing we could repeat them in the gym or on the playing field. We see a wonderfully natural speaker and wish that we could move people to the same level of ecstasy.

Ironically, the talented pianist, ball player, and speaker would probably insist that they need to improve to meet their own standards. They are not as good as they would like to be, yet we are able to see how wonderfully talented they are. How is this played out in your life?

It will do you no good to focus on the abilities that others have and you do not. You grow when you focus on your own talents, and practice them rigorously. Impress others with your skills and admire the skills of others. Your confidence will be contagious and inspiring.

I admire the talents of others but do not covet them.
Instead I realize that I am talented in many ways
and continually work to develop my own abilities.

DAY 218

*"If there is any secret of success, it lies in the ability to
get the other person's point of view and see things
from his angle as well as from your own."*

HENRY FORD

*E*ffective leaders focus on a clear vision and work to
convince others that it is in their best interest to help
achieve it. Remember this maxim if you expect others to "buy"
your ideas: People buy for their own reasons, not for ours.

Find out what motivates the people on your team. If you
want financing, learn what the interests of the financier are. If
you need people to work diligently, find out what makes them
work hard. See things from their point of view. Ask questions
before presenting your plans. Then present your plans in a way
that highlights the benefits for the people who are involved.
Never discuss your own gain. They do not care. Draw the picture
from their perspective. They will work harder to help you achieve
success if they see their own success through yours.

*I am able to see my vision through the eyes of those who will
help me achieve it. I position the vision in terms of
their own success rather than mine.*

DAY 219

---o---

"It is a rough road that leads to the heights of greatness."
LUCIUS ANNAEUS SENECA

*T*here are days when you feel like you are never going to get where you are heading. You move forward, yet there is an obstacle in your path that not only blocks your progress but also pushes you back with great force. People work against you, and you may not know it. Economics or new technologies force you to reconsider your plans and take an entirely new route. Politics throw you spinning off course at the most critical of times.

It is discouraging. Even the most resolute of leaders feel the desire to give up. When obstacles get in your way, remember your goals. See the vision more clearly. When you can visualize the end result, the means become less important. Obstacles are there. You cannot plan for them all. The only thing you can do is accept them with grace and acknowledge their inevitability. Then stubbornly move forward again. Your purposefulness will overcome any impediment that gets in your way.

I am relentless in the pursuit of my vision, in spite of the inevitable obstacles that block my path. My purpose gives me the strength I need to continually make progress toward my goals.

DAY 220

*"The more things change, the more
they remain the same."*

FRENCH PROVERB

We are bombarded with the change our society is facing. It is occurring at a rapid rate. The entire global village is involved. Power structures are evolving. We cannot predict where the change is taking us or to what degree our lives will be affected.

Even with all that is changing, human beings will remain just that. Human. Their needs remain constant. They need shelter. They need security. They need a sense of purpose. They need love. These factors will never change.

You can help others adapt more readily to the changes in the world by finding ways to assure them that their basic needs will be met. If they work with you, make them feel secure. Enliven their sense of purpose. Love them as you love all humanity. Your ability in understanding the constancy of human needs will help them accept and adapt to any change.

*Human needs for security, a sense of purpose, and love remain
constant. I continually take action to fulfill those needs
in those affected by the changes we face.*

DAY 221

---

*A*re you providing enough development to the people you lead so that they can effectively carry out your mission? How can you justify the high cost of training people who may use the new skills to find a better position somewhere else? And the cost—quality learning is expensive. With more emphasis on reducing expenses, training can seem like the most logical area to cut.

You absolutely cannot afford to cut back on training. Find ways to increase the developmental opportunities you provide. Your competitors are constantly changing the rules and redefining the game. You need to have skilled people to help you maintain and win market share. The fear that people will leave with the new skills is unjustified. Most people stay with organizations that care about their long-term development and viability. They leave when you do not provide them opportunities for growth. Keep their skills up to date, and they will keep you afloat.

*In spite of the cost, training is worth the investment. The education
and development of the people I lead is one of the surest
ways to maintain our growth.*

DAY 222

"There is more to life than increasing its speed."
MAHATMA GANDHI

*E*verything in life today seems to be happening at a faster pace. Telecommunication technology has increased the speed at which business is conducted. Regular use of overnight mail has increased impatience with traditional distribution systems even though they are faster than ever. On a personal level, our children are growing up faster, exposed to more knowledge (good and bad) than at any time in history.

Just because the technology is there does not mean that it has to be a metaphor for every aspect of your life. Slow down at times. Taking a walk in the country and actually looking at the vistas, the plants, and the wildlife cannot be sped up. The innocence of childhood should last longer and not be cut off prematurely just because the information is at your disposal. In business, it pays to take time to make critical decisions. Rushing into anything without thinking it through is dangerous. Slow down when possible and enjoy the experiences of life.

I take the time to make good decisions and enjoy life,
both personally and professionally.

DAY 223

"Things won are done, joy's soul lies in the doing."
WILLIAM SHAKESPEARE,
TROILUS AND CRESSIDA,
ACT 1, SCENE 2

Never sacrifice the here and now for a distant goal. The goal is important, but if you focus only on the goal, you will find that your life begins to feel empty and meaningless. You will work tirelessly in your zeal to complete the goal. When you arrive, you will probably look back and ask yourself, "Is this all there is?"

If you have not enjoyed the process of reaching the goal, the answer will be yes. If you do not maintain a sense of adventure, the answer will be yes. If you sacrifice your family or your own personal enjoyment, the answer of yes will be accompanied by bitterness and disappointment.

The process of achieving your goals is the fun part. Enjoy it wholeheartedly. Take time for yourself and your family. You only have now. Later, what you will find when you reach the goal is a horizon full of other goals and a path to them studded with more adventure.

*Today I will make it a point to enjoy the process of getting there.
I embrace the adventure both personally and professionally.*

DAY
224

---○---

"Iron rusts from disuse, stagnant water loses its purity, and in cold weather becomes frozen: even so does inaction sap the vigors of the mind."
LEONARDO DA VINCI

*O*ur bodies were designed to function effectively when active. The circulatory system relies on muscular movement to function correctly. The heart demands exercise that can only be done by increasing physical activity for a prolonged period at regular intervals. Muscles atrophy when not used, causing lack of stamina, aches, and pains.

Television, computers, telephones, Internet chat-lines, and many other conveniences combine to make our lives more sedentary. Be conscious of this and find time to exercise. You need to be in top mental condition to be a peak performer. Regular exercise not only makes you feel better, but it also increases the oxygen flow to the brain, helping you think better. Maintain your mental advantage by maintaining your physical condition.

Today I review my physical activity program to be sure my regimen provides the kind of conditioning that improves my mental as well as my physical condition.

DAY 225

---○---

*"Do not hold the delusion that your advancement
is accomplished by crushing others."*

CICERO

You cannot arrive at any destination without adequate roadways. Roads cannot be built by one person. It takes many people working together to plan and construct them. Trees have to be felled. Paths have to be cleared. Tunnels have to be built through mountains. Bridges have to be built over rivers.

Just as it takes many people working together to build a road, it also takes many people to accomplish your plans. Rather than trying to defeat those who get in the way of the path you are building, recruit them to help you. In order to defeat them, you have to burn bridges, which affects your journey as well as theirs. Do what you can to assure that you have as many people as possible clearing the path to your success, rather than waging battle over the routing or your right to construct it.

*I am skilled at recruiting others to help build the road that reaches
my vision. I never burn bridges. Instead I build alliances
and share the pathway to success.*

DAY
226

---○---

"Procrastination, the opposite of decision, is a common enemy which practically every man must conquer."
NAPOLEON HILL

*O*ne of the worst fears we can harbor is the fear of being wrong. It is manifested in the attitude that you must always be right and is the principal cause of procrastination. If you avoid making decisions, you will never be wrong.

As information technology becomes more advanced, leaders will have more data available to aid in the decision-making process. This is fine if you know when to stop investigating and take action. If, however, you are avoiding decisions for fear of being wrong, more information could be a problem. You will never have enough. With more information available you increase the probabilities of contradictory facts and advice. Do not become caught up in it. Set decision time lines. Complete them with confidence, and realize that not all decisions will be the correct ones. But failing to make decisions is *always* a bad decision.

I worry more about procrastination than about making bad decisions. I limit the amount of analysis, and I set time lines for decisions.

DAY 227

"I have always had a great respect for a Philippine proverb: 'Into the closed mouth the fly does not get.'"
THEODORE ROOSEVELT

As you move toward your vision and begin to accomplish your goals, the excitement can be overwhelming. You want to talk about your plans with everyone. Surely they will all be as excited as you are and share in your enthusiasm. You may be spurred to believe that the more people know about your plans, the more people will help you achieve them.

Not all people will be as excited about your vision as you are. Be cautious about whom you share your dreams with. Your hopes can be dashed by people who have contrary interests. Some may be jealous and work to sabotage your vision so that you cannot progress at a faster rate than they. Some may see themselves as your competitors. They believe they win by crushing your advance. They work to destroy your hopes. Do not let this happen. Talk about your plans only with those who will be supportive and have a genuine interest in you. The survival of your dreams relies on the discretion you apply to your communication.

To protect my visions and personal dreams, I share them only with those who have a genuine interest in me and my success.

DAY 228

---

*"You can't build a reputation on what
you're going to do."*

HENRY FORD

You can motivate the people you are leading by getting them excited about your vision and the things that you can accomplish together. Many will jump on board based on the clarity of your plans combined with your charisma. The force of your personal power is great.

You can convince people to work with you, but once convinced they have to see results. Prove your worth with action. You have to maintain your end of the bargain with all interest holders. You always get one chance. After that, people will work with you based on your accomplishments and not just promises. Work to keep your reputation spotless by providing a return on the investment of time, faith, and money that your backers and team members invest in your dreams.

*Today I will assess my actions to assure that I am acting to provide
an adequate return on the time, faith, and money that
others have invested in my dreams.*

DAY 229

"The truth is that all of us attain the greatest success and happiness possible in this life whenever we use our native capacities to their greatest extent."
SMILEY BLANTON

Never take a course of action purely for the sake of money, fame, or to please someone else. These motivations lead to failure. Even if you do not fail, you are not going to maximize your happiness.

You will always enjoy doing what you do best. If you are doing what you enjoy, you never have to force yourself into taking the action necessary to accomplish your goals. You will gladly do it. The irony is that if you concentrate your efforts on the areas where you have the most talents, money and fame will follow. If they do not, it will be from personal choice. As a leader, you are gifted with many talents that can help you achieve your dreams. Maximize their use. You will enjoy your vocation much more when it is also your avocation.

If I find that I am being bogged down with tasks that I do not like and am not good at, I immediately look for options to free me to use my own native talents and abilities.

DAY
230

*P*eople do not like inconsistency. One of the primary reasons why franchises have been so successful is that they have been able to assure consistent products. Whether you eat a Big Mac in Beijing, San Francisco, Des Moines, or Paris, you know what it is going to taste like. It is comforting. You always know what you will get for your money.

Leaders can learn from the franchise concept. To be successful, your message must be consistent no matter who the recipient is. Your purpose must never falter, unchanged by location, climate, or whim. Your ability to communicate effectively helps you control the uniformity of the message no matter who delivers it. As with hamburgers, people are attracted to consistency in leadership vision. Always be sure that your message is the same.

*Today I will take steps to be sure that my message
is constant no matter who is communicating it. I remain
consistent in my purpose and in the manner
in which I accomplish my objectives.*

DAY 231

"Some values are . . . like sugar on the doughnut, legitimate, desirable, but insufficient, apart from the doughnut itself. We need substance as well as the frosting."

RALPH T. FLEWELLING

*S*hare your values and discuss them regularly. Values guide your decisions. They help in determining the kind of work you will do, whose team you will join, who you will allow on your team, and how the work will be done. Values are not what you wish you had. They are not great concepts that will impress other people and build your reputation as a caring leader.

Values work for you only if you act on them on a daily basis. They irrefutably describe how you will act on your objectives. You must be able to describe in tangible terms what you are doing to accomplish your values. If you are unable to do so, reevaluate just what your values are. If you are not true to your values, it will be obvious to all around. Like sugar on a doughnut, the sweetness can fall away if not bound securely to the cake.

Today I will evaluate my values and ensure that I am tangibly acting upon them. I will do the same with my team and organizational values.

DAY
232

---○---

"Never tell people how to do things. Tell them what to do and they will surprise you with their ingenuity."
GEORGE S. PATTON

*M*anagers used to hold all of the information. Their job was exactly that—to manage. They told people what to do and how to do it. Then they supervised the completion of the tasks. Historically, effective leaders could never afford to follow the traditional manager model when dealing with people. They did not have time to closely supervise people. Their attention was focused on the big, strategic picture. They provided the "what." They let the people they led provide the "how."

Today, both leaders and managers have to follow this rule. If you add up the experiences of all those you lead or will lead, they would be significantly greater than yours. The people doing the tasks know how to be the most efficient. Leave them alone when it comes to the "how," and you will assuredly be rewarding them for the successful completion of the "what."

I realize that my job is to communicate the "what" of our objectives and vision. I let my team worry about the "how" and reward them for the results of their efforts.

DAY 233

"Luck? I don't know anything about luck. I've never banked on it, and I'm afraid of people who do. Luck to me is something else: Hard work—and realizing what is opportunity and what isn't."

LUCILLE BALL

Sheer luck is what it takes to win the lottery. The chances are minuscule. As a people, we are enchanted by luck. When someone achieves a great success, we call her lucky. She happened to be in the right place at the right time.

Luck has nothing to do with it, however. You are constantly involved in circumstances that could evolve into right-place or right-time scenarios. The key is to recognize when you are in a situation that could become an opportunity. People lucky in terms of success are really experts at analyzing their current situation and comparing it to their desired situation. When a match occurs, they act.

Pay attention to where you are. Look for clues that tell you an opportunity is underfoot. Then act. That is all the luck you will ever need and much more reliable than the lottery.

Today I will examine my current situation to see if there are opportunities that I have missed then take immediate action on them.

DAY
234

---○---

*E*veryone you lead is looking for opportunities to grow and develop. You want them to be. The initiative is energizing. You have a particular responsibility to help them grow. Your experience and perspective can help others move at a faster pace than you did. You paved the way. Give them the opportunity to continue on the path with you. Celebrate when they do so well that they pass you on the same road.

This is a particular challenge for small or downsizing organizations. You can still help people without having to promote them to higher positions. Growth is deeper than that. It comes from the soul. Mentor people. Teach them. Help them reach their own personal visions and goals. They have the need to grow. Find the resources to help them do it.

*I have a responsibility to help people grow and develop. Today I will
make it a point to find out someone's personal vision and
find the resources to help them achieve it.*

DAY 235

"My saving grace has been words. What did Lincoln wear? How did he feel? What did he eat? Nobody can tell you that. But they can tell you what he said."
NIPSEY RUSSELL

Communication is the backbone of any effective leadership strategy. You can have the greatest ideas in the world, but if you do not communicate them in a way that motivates others to help you achieve them, they will forever remain nothing more than ideas. You can have great values, but if you do not let other people know what your values are, they will never be able to align with them.

Tell people what you believe. Never hesitate to let people know what is in your heart. You will realize your vision only if you let others know what it is. People can make maximum use of your talents only if you tell them what they are. People can change behavior that is unproductive only if you confront them. Words are tools. Use them to build your effectiveness to the highest level.

Today I will make a special point to communicate more openly, which will help me build a lasting leadership program.

DAY 236

---

*"Mistakes are a fact of life. It is the response
to error that counts."*

NIKKI GIOVANNI

What is your reaction when you make a mistake? Many people try to cover it up. They may feel that it is not prudent to let anyone know of their failures. Sometimes the immediate reaction is to place blame. They will complain that there was not enough time to do things correctly. They may blame the customer or supplier for providing inadequate information. It could be the fault of the education system or government.

When you make mistakes, when things go terribly wrong, there is nothing you can do. You cannot make it right. You can study the causes so that it does not happen again. First, though, always ask yourself the question, "What could I have done differently?"

Taking personal responsibility helps prevent the problem from happening again. You also earn the respect of others as someone who is willing to accept accountability. Accountability is far more important in most people's eyes than your being right all the time.

*I take personal responsibility for the results of mistakes that
I make and encourage others to do the same with
my nonthreatening attitude.*

DAY 237

---○---

*"What a plague of one's thoughts, how great a rust of
the heart, to be jealous of another."*
THASCIUS CAECILLIUS CYPRIANUS

*H*ow do you react to another person's success? What
are your thoughts and feelings when someone does
something better than you or has a natural ability in an area that
is one of your weakest? It can be difficult to embrace another's
success without a tinge of resentfulness, especially if you are a
competitive person. Competition is learned at an early age, and
the feelings can get in the way when someone is better than you
are. Jealousy may manifest itself in language even when you are
trying to compliment someone. How many times have you told
someone that you "envied" her or him because of some accomplishment or some talent she or he had?

Negative feelings for someone else's accomplishments do nothing for you. They damage your own growth.

The next time you feel like saying you envy someone, tell that
person you admire her or him instead. Look for the positive attri-
butes of that person's success or abilities. Leverage a positive attitude
to maximize the potential of your own success and talents.

*I admire the success and talents of others. I make it a point to learn
from them, realizing that my positive attitude toward their
expertise helps propel me to great heights.*

DAY
238

---○---

Not enough people take a firm stand on their beliefs. They use all sorts of excuses. They say they do not have enough time. Who ever has enough time? They say they do not have enough money. Does anyone ever have enough money? They say they are too small and they could not make an impact. Are they not making an impact by not taking a stand and perpetuating the indifference?

Take stands. Firmly state your beliefs and take action on them. Encourage others to discard their apathy and replace it with caring. The world needs more caring. There are too many injustices in the world to ignore them. It is true that you cannot impact them all. You can choose an issue, however, and bring your passion to the forefront of it to bring about change. Act upon your concerns and let your example inspire others to do the same. Apathy has no place in a world with so many resources and so much potential.

*Today I will turn my compassion into passionate action
on an issue of great importance to me.*

DAY 239

"Don't pray when it rains if you don't pray when the sun shines."

SATCHEL PAIGE

*T*he demands on any leader's time are so great that sometimes fundamentals can be overlooked. After all, how do you prioritize? Family, work, civic organizations, community, and just plain keeping up with the latest advances in your field all demand your attention. It is a challenge to prioritize.

Usually, whoever is shouting the loudest gets the most attention. There are some areas that quietly go along day to day, without loud demands. The spiritual side of your life, God, or a higher power surrounds your life in ways that are mute to the ear, but not silent to observation. Notice that side of your life even when all other areas are demanding that you pay attention to them. Too often the intangible spirit is forgotten in the hubbub. The comfort it can provide will help you enjoy the good times and hectic times more fully as well as provide comfort when things are not going as well.

I remember the spiritual side of my life. When everything else is demanding my full attention, I still take the time to recognize my God or my higher power.

DAY 240

"Everything comes if a man will only wait."
BENJAMIN DISRAELI

*D*o you remember when you were a child waiting for a big day? Maybe it was your birthday or the last day of school. Remember the agony of waiting? Time seemed to crawl. Remember the road trips? You probably got in the car and within ten minutes began to ask if you were there yet.

It is funny how when people grow up time speeds up. Somehow, even though time is going faster, when it comes to your aspirations for yourself and others, time can again slow down to a snail's pace. We never seem to get over the childish impatience for important events.

Just as in your youth, you cannot rush the passing of time. You cannot make events happen faster than nature allows. If you are feeling anxious because of your wait, remember that you can only do so much. The unfolding is in the hands of the universe. Be patient. Wait. Just like that special holiday, things always arrive at the time they should.

Today I will make a point to table any impatience that I feel for anything that is outside of my control. When I feel anxious, I remember that all things happen at their own natural pace.

DAY 241

---○---

*"Only mediocrities rise to the top in a system
that won't tolerate wavemaking."*
LAURENCE J. PETER

*H*ow comfortable do you feel when people on your team directly challenge you and your leadership directives? If you are honest with yourself, you'll probably admit that you are a little disgruntled when someone does not seem to agree with your opinions and decisions. After all, you are a leader, which means others should naturally follow you. Even the most enlightened leaders feel that way from time to time.

Even if it is uncomfortable, you have to let people feel free to challenge. Confrontation is good when it is honest and well intentioned. You have to expect the same high degree of risk taking and courage that is expected of you in your leadership role. Otherwise you run the danger of being surrounded by people who tell you only what you want to hear. Encourage everyone to confront you at any time. You need their input even though it may be difficult to hear.

*Today I will remind the people in my life upon whose advice I depend
to confront me on any issue or situation. I accept their input
as a requirement to my success.*

DAY 242

---○---

"A universal human stupidity is the belief that our neighbor's success is the cause of our failure."
CHARLES VICTOR ROMAN

We live in a tremendously competitive society. Our heroes are often sports figures, renowned for their competitive prowess. Competition is so fierce in business that the focus of many is to keep up with the competition. Leapfrogging from one innovation to another has become a way of life.

If you are falling behind the competition, take your eye off them for a moment. Look toward your customers. You will inevitably find that you are not servicing their needs as effectively as someone else. It is not your competition's fault. It is yours. Take responsibility for your own losses and gains. Do so with an eye on the customers. Find out what they perceive their needs to be. Then service those needs and be the best at doing it. You will find that the competition will become less of an obstacle as a result.

I make it a point to be aware of my competition at all times, but I remain focused on my customers. By serving their needs better than anyone else, I maintain the competitive edge.

DAY 243

---○---

"I don't let my mouth say nothin' my head can't stand."
LOUIS ARMSTRONG

When life is over, and you have done your part to make the world somehow a better place, you are left with two things—self-respect and integrity. Always be true to yourself. If you dedicate your life to the service of ideals that you do not believe in, you will be miserable and unhappy. All the money in the world cannot buy back your integrity.

People look to you and listen to what you say. It is a natural part of your manner. Your influence goes deeper than you may ever imagine. Use the power you have carefully. Never compromise on your fundamental beliefs, even if it appears that the end will justify the means. That will never happen, because means that are contrary to your personal values perpetuate themselves through the end. It takes courage to stand for your beliefs. Live courageously, and you will live a full life with your honor intact.

If I do not agree with something because it is contrary
to my underlying values structure, I hold strong.
In this way I manage to keep my
self-respect and integrity intact.

DAY 244

*M*uch of your success depends on your own self-esteem. If you are proud of yourself and what you do, you will be able to hold your head high and do the things you have to do to be successful.

Feeling good about yourself comes from the inside. Although you may develop techniques to cover your emotions and true feelings so that the rest of the world is not aware of them, they do not go away. Even if you think you are covering up your emotions, they always shine forth in your behaviors. If you are not proud of what you are doing, you will not be able to force yourself to do well. If you are not proud of your accomplishments or of yourself, you will not be able to look in the mirror without seeing the person you truly are. Continue doing the things that reinforce your self-esteem and pride. No matter how costly, you must stop doing things that do not make you proud. The cost of continuing will always be greater than the cost of being true to yourself.

Today I will analyze the areas of my life where I am proud and areas where I am not proud. I will make the tough decisions necessary to assure my happiness and success.

DAY 245

"It is correct that there is no 'I' in the word TEAM.
But there is an 'M' and an 'E,' and together
they spell ME."

DONALD LUCE

*T*eam development within organizations is one of the most effective ways to adapt to the changes in the economy and society. The days of the generalist are waning. People are more specialized in their knowledge than ever before. There is a strong need for interdependence among individuals and departments. In order to remain competitive, the entire organization needs to be working together collaboratively.

Teaming used to mean that everyone subjugated individual needs for the good of the whole. You had to give up a substantial amount of your individuality. That never worked. Everyone contributing to a team effort brings unique talents and passions. Effective teams find ways to discover how each person can uniquely help to move toward the overall purpose of the organization. Find ways to celebrate the individual within the team, and you will soon be celebrating the accomplishments of the team.

I find ways to discover the talents and passions of individuals
on my team in order to understand how they
can uniquely contribute to our success.

DAY 246

*"If you're never scared or embarrassed or hurt,
it means you never take any chances."*

JULIA SOREL

No one likes to be embarrassed. Most people will go to great lengths to be sure that they are not hurt mentally. Actually most people take more care in guarding their psyche from damage than they do in guarding their bodies. If you are always putting yourself in a position of mental protection, you probably are not taking the risks you need in order to accomplish your objectives.

Generally, the greater the risk, the greater the opportunity. Where are you avoiding taking risks so that you can protect yourself from embarrassment? Is there someone you should call, except they might turn down your request? Should you take a stand in public that brings with it the risk of ridicule for your beliefs?

Take the risk and take the action. Your psyche will survive, and your vision will prosper.

*Today I will take action on an issue that I have avoided. I have
to risk feeling embarrassed, scared, or hurt in order to take
the necessary action to accomplish my goals.*

DAY 247

"The happiest moments my heart knows are those in which it is pouring forth its affections to a few esteemed characters."
THOMAS JEFFERSON

*M*any people look up to you. They admire you for your accomplishments. They admire the way you are able to get things done. They respect you for the stands you take.

When you receive positive reinforcement for what you do, it probably makes you feel very good. Sometimes it is a little uncomfortable to hear, but it helps you stand a little taller, work a little harder, and smile a little more easily.

When you are around people whom you admire, remember what it is like to hear positive reinforcement. Be prolific in your praise of others. Praise coming from a respected colleague or friend is the sweetest of all. When you commend others for a job well done, it lifts their spirits. When you acclaim their talents for all to hear, you help them to stand taller. You increase their self-respect. You motivate them to go on in a world that often offers only criticism. Be lavish with praise. Those you admire deserve to hear it directly from you.

Today I will make it a point to announce my admiration to those whom I admire.

DAY 248

"He who speaks first loses."

SUN-TZU

*T*he rest of the world could learn from Native American culture. It is a culture that values silence in human interaction, which sounds like a contradiction in terms. Silence—human interaction. In truth, much interaction takes place without words. Body language is the first thing that comes to mind. Eye contact is another. When you value silence, it gives you the opportunity to reflect on what the other person says and thinks before responding. When you measure your words carefully, you only speak the important.

Most people spend their listening time in a self-conversation deciding how to reply. They do not grasp the deeper meaning underlying the spoken word. Try silence in your interactions. Hear what the other person is saying without thinking of your reply.

You will find that silence increases your chances of hearing exactly what you need to hear to move any situation in the direction you need for it to go.

I understand the importance of silence as part of
my daily human interactions. Today I will focus
on fully developing the skill of silence.

DAY 249

---

*"Be scared. You can't help that. But don't be afraid.
Ain't nothing in the woods going to hurt you unless
you corner it, or it smells that you are afraid."*
WILLIAM FAULKNER

We can never totally conquer our fears. Fear is a natural human instinct. While at times it serves to impede our progress, it also serves to protect us. When fears block our opportunities to live to our fullest potential, we have to find ways to control them.

One way to control fear is to acknowledge it. Since it is a protective mechanism, it may be giving signals that you should heed. Once you analyze the fact that you are fearful, calculate the level of acceptable risk associated with your fear. It probably will not go away completely, even if you accept the risk. It will keep you aware. Just do not let it control your actions. Once you decide to move ahead, do so with all your force.

Go confidently into the unknown future. The future is yours. Do not let fear take it from you.

Fear has advantages in my life, and I acknowledge it as a protective mechanism. I control it and appear confident as I move with certainty into my future.

DAY 250

"Where there is no vision, the people perish."
PROVERBS 29:18 KJV

When you look at the state of leadership in the world today, what is really missing is vision. Few leaders articulate a clear, concise, and tangible vision of what their world would look like. Without vision the world just keeps on spinning, yet little progress is made.

As dangerous as having no vision is to have an old or stale vision. Vision is fluid. As you grow and mature, your vision will adapt around you. As the world changes, your vision must adapt to meet new challenges. As new people enter into your life and team, their personal visions need to come into alignment with yours.

Constantly revise your vision. It tells you where you are going. Be sure that you still want to go where you are heading. Then be sure everyone on board can see it as clearly as you. The survival of the world you would create relies on the constant adaptation and communication of what that creation looks like.

Today I will take steps to focus on my vision and make any adaptations necessary to keep it fresh and alive.

DAY 251

What have you done lately to actively solicit and understand the goals of those with whom you are closest? This includes your family, friends, and colleagues. The most important thing in the world to them is their own development. They may work hard to help you achieve your vision, but that labor will always take second place to their own needs.

Take some time and show a sincere interest in the needs of others. Ask them how you can help them achieve those needs. Give advice when asked. When others feel that they are fulfilling their basic needs and interests, they are more likely to help you fulfill yours. If you selfishly focus only on your own interests, they will do only as much as obligation necessitates. You need more than that. To get it, find ways to help them grow.

I am a caring leader and friend. Today I will take steps to clarify the needs of others so that I can help them in the same way I would like them to help me.

DAY 252

---○---

*"Makes you wonder. When I left St. Louis, I was
making five dollars a night. Now I'm getting $5,000
a week—for saying the same things out loud
I used to say under my breath."*
DICK GREGORY

You know the importance of listening to the people you work with and encouraging them to come to you with any problem. Your effectiveness hinges on your openness to listen to any kind of news, good or bad. It is painful to hear certain things, but it is better to hear them now than to be surprised by the results later.

How effective are you in doing the same thing with your mentors and leaders? Even if they are not as open to criticism and honest feedback as you are, it is your responsibility to give it. In most cases it is refreshing for a leader to hear contrary opinions from someone. Remember that as you expect the same from others, the contrary opinions you offer should be based in fact, with a recommended solution attached. Rather than being seen as negative, you will be seen as someone with the necessary fortitude to be tough and hold your ground.

*I am truthful with the people whom I consider my leaders and
mentors, just as I expect frankness from the people I lead. My
commitment to openness is a key factor in my success.*

DAY 253

"It is seldom in life that one knows that a coming event is to be of crucial importance."
ANYA SETON

*H*ow do you choose what in life is going to be important? There is no answer to that question. Do you attend every social function, because it may be the one that will bring with it a huge opportunity? Do you respond to every solicitation just in case you miss something? Do you go to every meeting? Obviously it would be impossible to do everything.

What you can do is consider every event that comes your way as a chance to find opportunity. Find out who will be there. Find out what will be discussed. Look for chances to put yourself into situations that will provide you the opening you need for opportunity. You will never know for sure which ones they are, but by analyzing the who, what, and why of each case, you will maximize your bet. Remember to be open to all the signals once you get there. You can lose the chance if you are not watching for it.

I will be more aware of the opportunities that may be present at each event I attend and maximize my chances to take advantage of them by thinking about the possible opportunities ahead of time.

DAY 254

"No man is able to progress when he is wavering between opposite things."

EPICTETUS

Nobody respects a leader who waffles. It is contrary to what we have come to expect from the strong people who lead us. If you do not take a stand on any issue, it boils down to indecision. Indecision of this sort is often caused by a desire to please everyone. You just cannot do that. On some issues, no matter what the decision you make is, you will create enemies. That is why leadership is difficult.

You may use the excuse that you are looking for compromise. You may actually be looking for it. You still need to make a decision on where you will stand. If you are negotiating a compromise, then you have to drive home the decision. As long as you waffle from one side to the other, nothing can get done. Never allow yourself to get caught in the waffle iron. It's a hot place to be, and you are bound to get burned.

It is natural for me to want to please as many people as possible, but in the end I courageously take stands and hold my ground on all important issues.

DAY 255

---○---

*"You cannot teach a man anything. You can only
help him discover it within himself."*

GALILEO

*T*hink of your role as a people developer for a moment.
Who around you needs help in order to work more
effectively or to reach their aspirations? In what areas do they
need help? They probably need help in areas where you are
unable to teach them. Perhaps you do not have the skills yourself.
Maybe you have a highly developed set of skills but do not have
the time to transfer all the knowledge.

That is all right, because you are a developer, not a teacher.
You only need to provide opportunities for development. Let
them discover the talents that are already inside. Pass along information and knowledge, but do not let it stop there. Provide
training. Encourage reading. Make sure that the person on the
receiving end has the opportunity to practice and use new skills
immediately. Provide development opportunities; then give the
other person the chance to grow into them.

*I continually remember that one of my primary roles is to develop
people. I find ways to provide knowledge and allow
the other person to develop.*

DAY 256

---

*"To be a great champion you must believe you are
the best. If you're not, pretend you are."*
MUHAMMAD ALI

*P*eople are attracted to confidence. Leaders with confidence exude an energy that excites. They carry their heads high. They walk with a self-assured gait. When they enter a room, heads turn to see. Yet they seldom notice the turned heads. They are not doing it for show. Perhaps that is what is so attractive. They are so directed that they do not even notice that others are noticing them.

Confidence is charismatic. It starts with self-belief and a healthy self-esteem. No one has the ability to do everything. No one can control all the circumstances of life, but you can control your own attitude. To exude confidence, believe in your ability to coordinate efforts that lead to accomplishment. Carry yourself in a self-confident way, whether or not you are confident at the moment. People cannot read your thoughts. They can see your comportment. Confident leaders attract and energize. Your charisma will move the world.

*I carry myself in a confident and poised manner at all times. My
charisma is exciting and energizing to all I encounter.*

DAY 257

*"The stakes . . . are too high for government
to be a spectator sport."*

BARBARA JORDAN

*T*he caring participation of the members of a democratic
society is what keeps government honest and focused
on the citizenry. Caring about government can be a daunting
task. After all, huge interests with a lot of money seem to control
the system. Corruption and scandal fill the newspapers of every
country. It is hard to believe that one person could really make
a difference.

The problem is, if you do not participate, who will? Many of
the large interests controlling things hedge their bets on the fact
that few individuals contribute to the governmental process. You
must pay attention to government. Your interests and the interests of those you serve and lead could be in jeopardy. Pay attention to the issues. Let your voice be heard. It will not be alone.
When joined with others like you who care about the same issues,
the forces add up. Participate in your government. It exists for
you.

*Today I set aside any cynicism I have regarding participating
in government. I look for opportunities to contribute
to the process and show that I care.*

DAY 258

"It's harder to defeat
Than it is to spell,
Revenge is not sweet,
It's bitter as Hell."

DUKE ELLINGTON

You cannot win every issue. Sometimes you will be beaten by someone. It would not be so bad if every defeat were the result of good intentions. That will never happen. Sometimes people win when they are selfish and self-centered. They may win on an issue just to further their own personal agendas. In their triumph, they may make matters worse by doing whatever they can to cause humiliation for you.

Focusing on revenge never helps. Manifestations of negative energy only drain you. Your counterpart may not even be aware of what you are doing or may actually take advantage of it by setting you up to look like the "poor loser." Accept any defeat with dignity and grace. Focus on your long-term vision.

You may go back into the battle. Do it to foster your goals, however, not to retaliate. Your win will be sweeter when it is done for a greater cause than your own redemption.

I make a point to concentrate on my goals and vision, even in the wake of defeat. My positive attitude and long-term focus are perceived as graceful and dignified to all observers.

DAY 259

*"Once you have been Number One, you can
never be satisfied with less."*

CHRIS EVERT

You are leading people and your organization to new frontiers. Your vision is the cement that bonds your team together. Being on top is an exhilarating place for a leader. It is also one of the scariest places. There is always someone ready to push you from your perch and take your place.

As you move toward dominance in any area, keep an eye out. The elation that comes with being on top blinds many leaders, making them feel indestructible. Ironically, you are often most vulnerable when you are in this position. As long as you are aware, and keep doing the things that got you to the top in the first place, your chances of staying there are excellent. Stay aware. Losing your superior position would be painful for you. Worse, it would be the height of demoralization for your team and organization.

I am constantly vigilant in my effort to be the best. Today I will analyze my strategy for being on the top as a leader and an organization and plan ways to maintain dominance.

DAY 260

Your ability to quickly learn new skills has helped you get to the level you currently enjoy. You are blessed with the aptitude to do many things well. Many of the opportunities that have come your way resulted from your ability to achieve a high level of competency fairly quickly. As much as this can be beneficial for you, it can sometimes be a curse.

When you can learn and develop quickly, you tend to believe that you can do anything. Because you are good at so many things, it may be difficult for you to admit that there are some areas where you do not have talents. Instead, you work to develop in areas that others could master in a shorter amount of time. Remember this when you feel inundated. Ask yourself whether there is someone who can do a job better than you can. If so, get that person to do it. This will allow you to concentrate on the areas where you excel. It will also free your time for the most important part of your duties—providing a vision and motivating others to follow your path.

*Today I will assess the functions I perform and determine whether
or not it makes sense for me to be personally involved. I freely
release to others the things that I do not do well.*

DAY 261

*"A ship in port is safe, but that is not
what ships are built for."*
BENAZIR BHUTTO

You cannot discover new oceans until you have the courage to lose sight of the shore. When traveling on the voyage associated with your vision, it is impossible to know what is over the horizon. There are many uncertainties. Like the ocean explorers centuries ago, you cannot be sure whether the world drops completely away where earth meets sky.

You will never know what lies beyond the horizon. The future cannot be forecast with complete accuracy. What you can be sure of is that the future seldom brings a crash into an abyss. Instead it gently slopes. You can glide over it, fearless of losing sight of the shore. As long as you are prepared for your journey, you will survive whatever the future brings. You will prosper, for treasure lies off in the distance, ready for you to find.

*I am inspired by the treasures the future holds for me. I fearlessly
dare to move ahead and take action on my vision
knowing that opportunity awaits my discovery.*

DAY 262

---

*"I believe racism has killed more people than speed,
heroin, or cancer, and will continue to kill
until it is no more."*

ALICE CHILDRESS

*D*iversity is one of the principal issues facing leaders today. As the world becomes smaller, we are all constantly in contact with more people from varying backgrounds. Different cultures, customs, religions, values, and work styles often clash. Misunderstandings result from the diversity that was never as evident as it is now.

You have a responsibility to manage the changes and accentuate the positive aspects of them. People look up to you. Your stand to provide opportunities for everyone with the necessary skills will set the pace for all who follow you. Your stand to promote diversity and prohibit discrimination will pave the way for a future of openness and understanding amongst all sectors of the community. Your positive attitude and encouragement in the adaptation process are vital.

*I take a stand to promote acceptance and understanding.
I encourage more diversity in all areas of my life.*

DAY 263

---○---

"I won't let people be neutral."
ANDREW YOUNG

Neutrality is safe. When you remain neutral about an issue, you never have to worry about backing up your belief. You, in essence, have no belief. Nonparticipation guarantees not having to confront anyone who disagrees. You just go on through life, letting the world happen as it will. Unfortunately, this also means you have to accept the consequences of your lack of viewpoint.

Never accept neutrality in yourself or others. Passion is the backbone of leadership. Blatant, unabashed passion is what motivates others, and it is what motivates you. Taking a stand for your beliefs and upholding them with all your energy opens doors to great gain. You will accomplish nothing if you forfeit your passions. Live passionately. Work passionately. Excitedly shout your opinions to everyone. Expect the same from everyone. Your embrace of passion and opinion will move more people than anything.

I am a passionate leader, dedicated to motivating others and accomplishing great things. Today I will communicate my opinions more strongly and live my passions in all of my actions.

DAY 264

---

*"Make it a practice to keep on the lookout for novel and
interesting ideas that others have used successfully.
Your idea has to be original only in its adaptation
to the problem you are working on."*

THOMAS ALVA EDISON

You do not have to reinvent the wheel in order to develop one with better traction. Hundreds of opportunities pass before your eyes every day. In order to grasp hold of those opportunities and do something with them, you must first see them.

Look for areas not being served by existing products or services. With a little adjustment from the current situation, you can fill a need. Most successful new ideas are gradual innovations. This goes for your leadership style as well as for products and services. There is no new way to lead. There are things we can learn from the old ways, and we should make gradual improvements. Adapt your style to meet new needs just as you would adapt a product or a service for your organization. The acceptance will be greater, and you will not have to dedicate so much energy inventing something new.

*I am open to innovation by constantly looking for new needs
that could be filled with existing products and services.*

DAY 265

"We are not creatures of circumstances; we are creators of circumstance."
BENJAMIN DISRAELI

What have you done lately to create something new in your life? We are here to create. It is part of our natural instinct. Unfortunately, it is easy to get caught up in the day-to-day routine and go with the flow. Because of our natural predilection toward creating, most people find life unsatisfying when they allow themselves to be pushed by the current.

Leaders are constantly on the lookout for new opportunities. Keep in mind that the opportunities do not happen to you. They just present themselves. Your responsibility is to create something with them. Manipulate opportunities to fit your needs and the needs of others. If you do not do something with them, they disappear. The next time you see an opportunity, create something out of it. It takes effort to escape from the normal routine, but the personal satisfaction is worth it.

I am aware of opportunities that surround my every move. Today I will take action to create something out of an opportunity.

DAY
266

---○---

*"The most valuable executive is one who is training
somebody to be a better man than he is."*
ROBERT G. INGERSOLL

You will not always be in the same position you are
now. You probably do not want to be. Many leaders
make the mistake of working to make themselves as irreplaceable
as possible. In today's insecure environment, self-protection of
this sort is understandable. It is not practical, however.

You have a responsibility to yourself and to those who will
follow in your steps to ensure their readiness to take your place.
Your job is not to do everything better than those you lead. You
have to teach them and develop them to their fullest capacity.

It is extremely rewarding to watch someone grow and prosper
as a result of your teaching. Lead by teaching others, and you
will always have someone to put in your place when you move
on to better opportunities.

*Today I will make it a point to assess the needs of those around me
and the ways that I can help them to become even better than I.*

DAY 267

"He who rejects change is the architect of decay. The only human institution which rejects progress is the cemetery."
HAROLD WILSON

You may be willing to change to adapt to new times, but are the people you influence willing to do the same? Certainly one of your greatest challenges as a leader is to manage the change process and to motivate others to accept and adapt to it. Many of the changes in organizations threaten the people associated with them. Not just the employees are afraid; their families, service providers, vendors, and customers are too.

Your challenge is to show these people what they have to gain from the changes you try to implement. Listen to them. Communicate freely. Sometimes it is not the message that causes resistance; it is the lack of a message. You cannot guarantee that everyone will be happy with changes. You can, however, help them understand the reasons and show them how they can benefit. If there are no apparent benefits, you can at least help them make the transition go more smoothly.

Today I will pay special attention to the changes that are affecting the people I influence. The most important thing I can do is communicate the benefits and listen to their concerns.

267

DAY 268

"Which of you, intending to build a tower, sitteth not down first, and counteth the cost?"

LUKE 14:28 KJV

You are blessed with the incredible power to be able to create anything you want. You may choose to build a castle in the sky or a shack by the sea. Both are possible. Both have their appeal.

The important word is *choice*. Because you have a choice, you must decide what the costs of your decisions are. You will have to pay a dear price regardless of the decision. No matter what you choose, you will have to give up something to get it. The question is, Which things are most important? What will be the effect of your dreams on your family? What will be the effect on your free time? What about your self-esteem? What is the financial cost or gain? What about your soul? Know the price you will pay for whatever you dream. Weigh it against the benefit. Is it a good value? The answer is in your heart.

A cost is associated with any decision that I make.
Today I will review those costs to confirm
in my heart the direction I have chosen.

DAY 269

---○---

*B*efore you can help others, you have to know the areas in which you need help. Before you can enlist the help of others, you have to know how you can help them. Before you can dovetail your talents with the talents of others, you have to know your own talents. Before you can ask others to follow your vision, you have to know what your vision is.

These are simple premises and are easy to grasp intellectually. The difficult part is to put the ideas into practice. Every leader has to continually go through a process of self-discovery. Inventory your strengths and needs. They change regularly. We tend to make these evaluations of others naturally. For some reason, it is more difficult to do it with ourselves.

Who are you? What are your strengths and needs? Know yourself first, and it will be easier to know those whom you lead.

As an effective leader, I inventory my own abilities, beliefs, and needs on a regular basis. Today I will make an effort to know myself better than I do now.

DAY 270

---○---

"Invest in the human soul. Who knows, it might
be a diamond in the rough."
MARY MCLEOD BETHUNE

*O*rganizations and leaders usually realize the importance of investing in the people who are critical to their success. The investment is usually in the technical skills necessary to do jobs or tasks more effectively. Product training, market training, and management skills training all fall into this category.

We often ignore investing in the soul of the individual. By providing opportunities for individuals to develop their internal selves, leaders help them discover their true motivations and happiness. Looking inside, they can touch in with their values, their principles, and their talents. They can find their passion. They can discover their compassion.

This spiritual side of an individual is just as important as the technical skills. Individuals at peace with themselves can maintain the focus they need to do their jobs effectively. They contribute because they have defined and developed who they are as much as what they do. Helping others find their own soul is one of the most penetrating gifts a soulful leader can give.

I work with my associates to find tangible ways to invest
in their souls and help them grow as people.

DAY 271

*"I am an optimist. It does not seem too much
use being anything else."*
WINSTON CHURCHILL

Think for a while about the messages you process on a
daily basis. Almost everything you are exposed to is
negative. The news media focuses primarily on tragedies. They
tell you that the economy is in a tailspin, government is failing,
and people are evil.

It is not hard to understand why it is so difficult to maintain
a positive attitude. No sooner are you optimistic about something
than someone tells you why it will not work. You get a great
idea, and you can find a hundred reasons why it is a bad idea.

People who accomplish great things ignore the negative messages. They look for reasons why something can be done rather
than why it cannot. Of course, they analyze to be sure that they
are being realistic but then plow full speed ahead with enthusiasm. Anything is possible. Ours is a world of abundance. Distance
yourself from the negative messages you are bombarded with daily.

I am a faithful optimist, able to achieve any great thing.

DAY 272

"Many persons have a wrong idea of what constitutes true happiness. It is not attained through self-gratification but through fidelity to a worthy purpose."
HELEN KELLER

*P*eople spend so much effort trying to be happy. They play games, they go on trips, they spend time with friends, they take antidepressant medication. Still they have trouble attaining a feeling of true satisfaction. The joy of being eludes them.

People are happiest when they are occupied with activities related to a purpose that is higher and greater than themselves.

A common characteristic of centenarians is that they are active and involved in purposeful daily activity, whether church, volunteer activity, or family. They think of the future. They are concerned about helping. They are happy when they feel as if they are contributing. The next time you question whether you are happy enough, question whether you are serving a purpose that is greater than you are. Such activity brings great satisfaction and joy.

My happiness does not hinge on what the world can give me but rather on what I can do for the world. I serve the world with great purpose and enthusiasm.

DAY 273

"If a man insisted always on being serious, and never allowed himself a bit of fun and relaxation, he would go mad or become unstable without knowing it."

HERODOTUS

When was the last time you did something really off the wall? If you are like most people, you get more serious as a result of all your responsibilities.

Nuttiness and fun help you survive the seriousness and the pace of today's environment. No one ever said you could not laugh a little. It is time you learned a new joke. Maybe you need to get away for a long weekend. How about a humor workshop? Open a bottle of champagne for no other reason than to celebrate the sound it makes when the cork pops out. Laughter and smiles are the most effective energy boosters you can get without a prescription. Do something today to bring them out and create more bustle in your life as a result.

I am able to see the funny side of my day-to-day activities. Today I will act on that funny side and bring more smiles and laughter into my life.

DAY 274

*"The desire of bettering our condition comes with us from
the womb and never leaves us until we go to the grave."*
ADAM SMITH

You are surely well aware of the desire to better your condition. Most leaders work tirelessly in an effort to move ahead, to make a more comfortable or stimulating life. As you move in the direction of making the conditions surrounding your life better, it is important to realize that everyone around you has the same desires.

If you can find ways to help your associates better their conditions, you will go a long way toward motivating them. They will help you as long as they know it is reciprocal. Yet, if they do not see opportunities for advancement or greater challenges, they will leave. Even if they do not leave physically, they will leave psychologically. Do not let that happen. You have the power to help them find ways to grow. By helping them grow, you will find that your own growth comes more easily.

*Today I will look at those whose lives revolve in my sphere. There are
ways I can help them better their conditions or opportunities,
and I readily take action to do so.*

DAY 275

*I*t would be nice if we could develop a concrete vision
and purpose statement, hang it on the wall, and use it
for years to set our direction. Nicely worded and neatly packaged,
it would motivate us and others, keeping us on the path to
success.

The world is not a static place. It is continually changing.
Why, then, would we keep our view of the future the same?

Your vision and purpose must be fluid. You are always learning
new things. Variables appear that you did not know about when
you established your vision. Revise your vision frequently to be
sure you are heading in the direction you want to be going.
Check your purpose on a regular basis. Constantly ask yourself
if you still want to be headed where you determined earlier that
you wanted to go. Your vigilance over your vision assures that
you will reach even greater heights than you thought.

*Today I will take time to rethink my vision and purpose. I will take
action to set new directions where indicated.*

DAY 276

---○---

*"Alas! The journey of life is beset with thorns
to those who have to pursue it alone."*
ALEXANDRE DUMAS JR.

*A*re you leveraging your network of friends, colleagues, and associates as effectively as you could be? Your network is one of your most effective tools for accomplishing your vision. Through the people in it you can find guidance, support, direction, and experience.

You have a limited quantity of energy when you work alone and rely only on yourself. When you rely on your network, you can generate energy that replicates itself within the various networks to which members of your network belong. Capitalize on the contacts you have. They will help you. Let them know that at the same time you are willing to dedicate your talents and contacts to help others achieve their visions.

*My network of contacts want to be of great assistance in helping
me reach my goals and aspirations. Today I will find
new ways to capitalize on their presence.*

DAY 277

"Nothing splendid has ever been achieved except by those who dared believe that something inside them was superior to circumstances."

BRUCE BARTON

*M*uch of your growth as a leader has probably hinged on your ability to motivate people to move toward a goal. Your ability to work out compromises has helped to increase your reputation as a coalition builder. You have the capability of getting people to see the advantages of doing things your way or seeing the world through your eyes.

There are times when you cannot reach a compromise. It may not be in someone's best interest to cooperate fully with your plan. For someone accustomed to being able to convince others and please them most of the time, this can be a difficult proposition.

Remember that even the most popular leaders have enemies. What those leaders recognize is that there are some issues where not everyone will be pleased. It is a natural circumstance of taking strong stands. When you accept that fact, you increase your opportunities for growth regardless of how painful it may be to not always have full acceptance of your plans.

I take risks and take stands when necessary for the greater good, even though not everyone is in agreement.

DAY
278

*"Everybody can be great . . . because anybody can serve.
You don't have to have a college degree to serve. You don't
have to make your subject and verb agree to serve. You only
need a heart full of grace. A soul generated by love."*
MARTIN LUTHER KING JR.

A leader's life is dedicated to service. You work to serve
your organization in the most effective way possible
so that it can enjoy continued growth. You work to serve those
whom you lead so that they can develop their talents, grow as
people, and work in service themselves. You serve your family so
that they can live a comfortable and meaningful life.

You have the advantage of being able to use your unique
abilities and influence to serve your community also. A tremendous number of social ills need your urgent attention. Make a
difference by serving the public so that people you do not even
know can benefit from a life with greater hope and opportunities.
Influence your organization to support social causes. Encourage
those you lead to give back to society. Your action will have a
great impact on the world.

*I am motivated to use my unique abilities and influence to make
a difference within my community. Today I will take action to
make an impact in an area that particularly troubles me.*

DAY 279

*"Men tinged with sovereignty can easily feel
that the king can do no wrong."*
PAUL DOUGLAS

*F*ew people have larger egos than leaders. After all, leaders wield a tremendous amount of power, both personal and positional. They have the ability to determine whether people will continue in a job or a position. The decisions leaders make can earn or lose tremendous quantities of money.

All that power can easily go to your head. People respect you and tell you how good you are. They often do so whether they mean it or not because you are the leader and can mete out favors. The key is not to believe it all. The world is a tenuous place, and leaders are at the top of a very unstable mountain. There is always someone willing to knock you off the top. Stay in touch with your humanity. Be willing to compile and maintain support. Be willing to ask for help and reinforcements when you need them. Your determination to keep your power in perspective is the most effective way of being able to maintain it.

*I keep my power in perspective by focusing on my humanity
and my connection with my support group.*

DAY 280

---○---

*A*s a leader you will find a great deal of competition for your position. No matter how valid your ideas and how compelling your vision, there are always people who have contrary ideas and vision. They will do what they can to tumble you from your spot of leadership so they can fill it and implement their plan.

Your position often relies as much on marketing as on ability. You have to have both. You can be the best leader in the world, but if others do not know what you do or how well you do it, your position is in jeopardy. Market yourself. Keep others informed of your progress and your accomplishments. In this manner, protect yourself from others who would have your position.

*Today I will take action to be sure that my contribution
and competence are clearly visible. My vision relies
on my ability to market myself as well as my ideas.*

DAY 281

---○---

*"No life grows great until it is focused,
dedicated, disciplined."*

HARRY EMERSON FOSDICK

*S*elf-discipline is one of the key characteristics leading to success. There are temptations around every bend as you stride along the path to success. We are motivated by pleasure and pain, making it difficult to maintain long-term discipline when confronted with short-term enticements.

Most people will be tempted to lose focus when confronted with something that is more pleasurable to them than the current pain they experience on their journey. This includes such things as enjoying an unplanned conversation with someone rather than doing a tedious task or failing to take time for daily reflection in favor of the short-term pleasure of sleeping in fifteen minutes longer. Lack of discipline feels pleasurable for a while. What you have to remember is the discomfort of not reaching your goals or not being as effective as you could be, or losing your commanding leadership presence. A disciplined life brings success and more lasting pleasure than the temptations that get in your way.

*I stick to my commitments regardless of the temptations that offer
short-term pleasure. Today I will make an added effort
to maintain control of my time and my activities.*

DAY 282

*"Power . . . is not an end in itself, but is an instrument
that must be used toward an end."*
JEANE KIRKPATRICK

The more power you have, the more you can accomplish. You call the shots. You can determine who will be involved in a project and who will not. You can choose the parameters. Power, while a useful tool for a leader, can become addicting. It is tempting to use your power for illicit reasons.

It is not the goal of leadership to maximize power. If that becomes your goal, power will remain elusive. The only way to gain more power is to competently work toward a purpose that is higher than yourself. You gain power when others see the benefit of having you in charge. Power comes when you have a reason to use it.

As you become more powerful as a result of your achievements, your responsibility to fulfill a higher purpose will increase. Power comes to those who can and will use it as a tool to serve others, not as a tool to serve themselves.

*My power base continues to increase as I constantly check my vision
and purpose and work toward serving a greater good.*

DAY 283

---○---

*T*he amount of time needed to complete any project is directly related to the amount of time you have dedicated to it. You have the ability to do more than you are doing now, if you are organized, disciplined, and directed.

As long as you take action to begin something new, energy will come to propel it to completion. In the end, you are not measured by the amount of time you spend in your office. You are measured by the objectives you fulfill.

If you are having trouble fulfilling all your objectives, maybe you are letting the project fill the amount of time you have dedicated to it. Think of how much time is wasted during your day. If you would effectively use that time, you would find an infinite number of hours open up to you. You could then fill them with leisure or any other activity that will help you progress toward your vision.

I work efficiently, competently, and in a disciplined manner, which increases the amount of time I have to work toward my vision.

DAY 284

*T*he race is on for organizations to become learning organizations. This type of organization places a high value on the development of new skills in order to compete effectively in a changing environment. They provide opportunities for employees to learn skills that make them more productive as well as protect their positions in the workforce.

Businesses can only become learning organizations if learning is valued by the people in them. You play a key role in the future as you encourage an atmosphere of excitement and opportunity around learning. Set the example yourself. You can benefit from skill development as much as those who work for you. By assuring that you yourself grow, you can more effectively talk about the benefits of learning within the organization. There is always something new to learn. Learning protects not only those whom you lead, but also your position as a leader.

Today I will take action to assure that my own skills are up to date
and to encourage those I lead to do the same.

DAY 285

*O*ur lifeblood is often data. So much of it is available to us. You would think that with all the information available on which to base decisions, it would be easier to do and people would make better decisions.

All the information in the world cannot take away from the pure gut instinct that a leader uses to make decisions. It is never possible to have all the information you need, because the one thing we can never know for certain is the future. Information only provides details about the past. Your advantage is in the development of and reliance on your intuition. If a decision feels bad, it probably will be.

Nobody knows exactly how intuition works. It really does not matter. What matters is your acceptance of the role of feeling in the decision-making process. In the end, that is what you will base most of your conclusions on anyway.

To make good decisions, I am careful to analyze as much information as necessary, but in the end, I trust my intuition to guide me in the right direction.

DAY 286

*L*eading is a serious business. People's lives depend on the decisions you make. The future of your organization hinges on your abilities. Your family would not have the security and comfort it depends upon without you.

No matter how much you plan to deal with your responsibilities, random things will get in your way. As much as you are visualizing in one direction, others are visualizing in another. Even worse, you are constantly affected by people who have no vision or plan, yet when your paths collide, they can send you reeling off course. Laugh when these things happen. Life is more enjoyable when you can see the funny side of things. People are attracted to leaders who do not take everything seriously. An ambiance of fun makes recovering from the little and big failures easier and motivates others as well as you to jump back on course and aim again for the vision you develop.

Today I will make it a point to look for the funny side of each step and misstep I, and those I lead, take. An ambiance of enjoyment adds energy and excitement to the vision.

DAY 287

"*Courage is the ladder on which all the other virtues mount.*"
CLARE BOOTHE LUCE

The list of virtues that make great leaders is long. You are measured and judged by your virtues. They set you apart from all others. For all the competition in the world, it is most difficult to compete with someone whose actions are based on virtue. Your own sense of integrity assures that you live up to them.

Apart from integrity, a leader most needs courage. It is perhaps the one thing that is most difficult to find in leaders. Courage lets you speak up when something is wrong. It does not matter what happens to you as a result; if it is right, a courageous person says so. Courage keeps you honest. It is the base that assures you will act on all your virtues. It keeps fear at bay by sheer force of will. Whatever your actions, make sure that you take courageous steps. Your reputation and self-esteem rely on it.

Courage helps assure that I complete even the most difficult of my goals. Today I will take courageous steps where I may have been limited in the past by fears and insecurity.

DAY 288

"We trained hard—but it seemed that every time we were beginning to form into teams, we would be reorganized. I was to learn later in life that we tend to meet any new situation by reorganizing; and what a wonderful method it can be for creating the illusion of progress while producing confusion, inefficiency, and demoralization."

PETRONIUS, A.D. 65

*I*n today's environment, the way to fix any problem seems to be to restructure. Moving people in, moving people out, and getting rid of people form the basis for most restructuring.

The problem is that seldom is a systems approach used when restructuring. Instead groups are reorganized as a reaction to an emergency. For the short term, there appears to be progress, but inevitably another problem crops up somewhere else in the line as a result of the patch-up work.

To work on problems, look for the root causes of the problems you face. Determine the process for eliminating the problem with the system before you rearrange the parts of the system. This prevents problems from surfacing elsewhere in the organization. It keeps morale higher and in the end adds to the efficiency you need to be competitive in today's climate.

I resist efforts to restructure and react to problems without analyzing the root causes of the problem. I force a systems approach to all problem solving.

DAY 289

"Some problems are so complex that you have to be highly intelligent and well informed just to be undecided about them."

LAURENCE J. PETER

*I*t takes a lot of courage to make the difficult decisions you are faced with. Sometimes it takes the same amount of courage to not make a decision. The skill does not lie only in making a decision. Real leadership skill lies in developing excellent judgmental abilities so that you know when to cut off the analysis and make a decision, and when to keep on analyzing.

Judgment skills can be practiced and developed. They come with keeping up with the trends in your field. It also helps to learn to follow your intuition.

Your good judgment hinges not only on your own analytical abilities, but also on the willingness to share the information and decision analysis responsibilities with others. You can never have all the information you need, but you do need to make sure that you have enough to make a rational decision. It is a rough tightrope to walk, but you have the ability to do it with ease.

Today I will take steps to increase my judgment skills and put them into practice.

DAY 290

*L*eaders are not known to be the most patient of all human beings. Your world is full of demands. You have a vision of the way the future should be. You have the ability to cause things to happen, to dream a dream and create what you saw in the dream.

It is difficult to accept at times, but the rest of the world goes on spinning while you dream your dreams and plan for their completion. You will never have total control of the timing. Myriad variables must come together in order for your vision to take place. While you can try to guess how long it might take to complete your vision, you cannot control many of the factors that delay it.

Have patience when things do not happen as quickly as you would like. Do not allow yourself to become discouraged when things take longer than you like. Too many people stop acting on their dreams just when they are ready to happen.

I determine realistic expectations regarding the completion of my dreams. I am persistent in my efforts even when things take longer than I would like.

DAY 291

―――○―――

"Genius is one percent inspiration and ninety-nine percent perspiration."

THOMAS ALVA EDISON

*F*or many the dream is enough, and that is all they do. The world is full of geniuses who can at an instant look at any situation and see the possibilities that it holds. Even though they see the possibilities, nothing ever happens. They do not have the fortitude or spunk to see their ideas through to completion. They are smart enough to know that there is no substitute for hard work and diligence in the pursuit of a dream.

When you develop your vision about the way things should be, remember that there are many steps ahead that you must take to make it happen. Find your satisfaction in the pursuit of the dream rather than its accomplishment. That will give you the fortitude you need to continue through the difficult times when no one but you believes in the possibilities and when the forces of nature seem to work against you. Eventually you will accomplish your goal. Be willing to toil in order to do so.

I gain my personal satisfaction as much from doing the things necessary to complete my goals as from their completion. Today I commit to working even harder to build my dreams.

DAY
292

---

*"The shoe that fits one person pinches another; there is
no recipe for living that suits all cases."*
CARL JUNG

Your vision compels you more than most any other
thing in your life. That is one of the things that makes
you special as a leader. Your passion is the driving force in your
life, and because of it you will be able to continually accomplish
even greater things.

As difficult as it is to accept, the vision that is so compelling
to you may have only a moderate effect on someone else. Not
everyone is able to see the possibilities that the future holds as
clearly as you. Still, you need the cooperation of many in order
to reach your goals. Focus on what is important to others when
you are persuading them to move in your direction. What motivates them? What are their compelling dreams and desires? When
you touch them, and incorporate them into yours, you have the
power to make your dreams happen.

*My vision is bright and fills my life with a compelling desire
to create. I find the benefit for others
that motivates them to help me.*

DAY 293

---○---

*"Part of teaching is helping students learn how to tolerate
ambiguity, consider possibilities, and ask questions
that are unanswerable."*
SARA LAWRENCE LIGHTFOOT

*L*earning does not end when someone finishes formal
education. It takes on a new form. It begins again.
Formal education focuses on rote instruction designed to equip
students with a certain degree of cultural literacy and introduce
them to the basic concepts. Testing is basic, and there are usually
answers. Seldom is it correct to disagree with the professor.

Because of the way the education system is designed, the people you lead have certain culturally reinforced fears about discovering, exploring, and questioning. You are the teacher in the
school of real life. Turn the system upside down with your insistence on independent thought and reasoning.

Creativity comes from a willingness to see things from a different angle. It comes from feeling free to ask questions of authority.
By encouraging and rewarding behavior that may be new to many
of those you lead, you have the opportunity to teach them for the
first time what it means to be creative while still being productive.

*I stimulate an environment of creativity by encouraging question
asking and the exploration of new ideas.*

DAY 294

"There are two kinds of talent, man-made talent and God-given talent. With man-made talent you have to work very hard. With God-given talent, you just touch it up once in a while."

PEARL BAILEY

You can develop any skill needed to do a task. You have some skills that are really natural talents. You probably do not even remember learning them. They have always been easy. If you are like most people, you naturally gravitate toward your natural talents. They take less work. They are more interesting to you.

The people you lead are working within the same dynamic. They will gravitate toward tasks that maximize the utilization of their natural talents. They put off doing tasks that cost them an excessive amount of effort. Just knowing this helps you to understand why some people are unhappy with their positions. If they are not utilizing their natural talents and are using skills that require too much energy, they feel stressed and overworked. Help them find the balance. Then encourage them to work hard to develop the skills that are difficult. No matter how difficult, once a skill is learned it becomes easier and more automatic with practice. Getting over the learning curve is the worst part.

I understand the need to help people work as much as possible utilizing their natural talents, and I also encourage them to develop all the skills necessary for them to become effective.

DAY 295

Your plan is impressive. What you say you can do is phenomenal. When you speak, your passion excites others and makes them want to do whatever is necessary to help you reach your goals. You can capture imaginations and show people how high they can soar.

Your credibility, however, does not come from the vision or the dream. It does not come from your ability to excite people. Credibility comes from making things happen. No matter how much your passion inspires people, what really gets them to believe you and stand behind you is your action. When you do what you say you want to do, you gain trust and respect. More people are willing to jump on board when they see that you are actually making the dream happen. Take action on your dreams. Making them happen is how you really generate excitement.

My credibility hinges on my ability to take action and make my vision come to life. Today I will concentrate on taking action on something that in the past I have only talked about.

DAY 296

"Consumers are statistics. Customers are people."
STANLEY MARCUS

Whether you are a leader in a profit or nonprofit organization, you have customers. You have customers when you lead a group of Girl Scouts. Those customers are no less important than the customers of a major industrial company. Leaders focus much of their energy on the customers and how to fulfill their needs.

Customers are people who use your service or product. They are your reason to exist. They pay the way, so to speak. Who are your customers? The surest way to gain customer loyalty is to have a satisfied customer. Although this sounds simple, it is a truth that few people follow.

What are you doing to fulfill customers' needs? To ensure your survival and growth, put yourself in your customers' shoes. Ask yourself what you would need from yourself or your organization if you were the customer. Then honestly answer whether you are providing what they want. If you are not, take action immediately. Your focus on your customer keeps you in top form in the competitive race.

Today I will focus on customers to ensure that I am doing everything possible to understand their needs.

DAY 297

—◯—

*"Talk that does not end in any kind of action
is better suppressed altogether."*
THOMAS CARLYLE

You probably attend more meetings than you would like. As the environment in which we work becomes more team oriented, it is a natural progression that we will need more meetings in order to reach consensus on decisions. Meetings are also taking new forms. Technology has allowed meetings to take place via telephone, via satellite video, and via computer link-up. Meetings do not have to be face-to-face anymore.

It is only natural that you will encounter resistance to the increased number of meetings. Most people are feeling a time squeeze as it is, without piling more meetings on top of their duties. You can have a great influence on countering resistance by doing one thing. Make sure all meetings you sponsor end with action plans. When people turn talk into action and take responsibility for accomplishing tasks as a result of the meeting, they are more willing to participate.

*The importance of coming to closure on issues in meetings
and developing clear action steps on items discussed
cannot be overemphasized.*

DAY 298

────○────

*"By appreciation we make excellence in others
our own property."*

VOLTAIRE

*T*hose with whom you work spend a lot of their energy making your vision come true. When your vision is compelling enough and you communicate it with enough passion, others help you achieve it because they want to. They want to see you successful. Being part of something that is exciting and dynamic is very rewarding for everyone.

Be careful to avoid getting so caught up in the vision that you forget the efforts of those who are making it possible for you to achieve it. Appreciation is one of the greatest motivators. Sometimes your appreciation is all someone needs to put forth just that little extra effort to make your dream a reality. Acknowledge their help frequently not only to them, but also to others. Make them a part of the project, not just a cog in the wheel. You owe it to them. They are helping you fulfill your dreams.

*Today I will take steps to acknowledge others with the same
passion I use to pursue my dreams.*

DAY 299

---○---

O nce you have your vision set and your purpose clearly stated, the work has just begun. By clarifying your direction, you set a whole chain of events into play that reverberates in many directions. Be aware of every opportunity that comes your way. Be open to the underlying meanings of what people say when you talk to them. Watch for signs that you should pursue a certain direction.

Most important, never miss the chance to uncover an opportunity. Opportunities are not always in your regular day-to-day environment. Search for them. Add new people to your network of contacts. Pick up the telephone and call someone you do not know but would like to get to know. Go to meetings where you will find other people like you. Attend classes and conferences. Read the newspaper regularly. Follow your trade press. If you want success, you must look for opportunities. They present themselves only if you are in a position to see them.

Opportunities present themselves to me when I am in a position to see them. I will take steps today to develop new contacts to add to my network and to expand my regular horizons.

DAY 300

Some of the problems we face as inhabitors of the earth appear insurmountable. We are besieged with hunger, poverty, famine, drugs, crime, global warming, the breakdown of the family, high school drop-out rates, teen pregnancy, declining values, and on and on. So many factors influence each individual problem that logic would dictate that no one individual could possibly have an effect on anything.

You can have an effect, though. Your leadership can play a crucial role. The most damaging problem we face may be defeatism. Some people want to throw their hands in the air and quit. Finding ways to use their hands to solve problems would be more effective. We are on Earth only for a short time. We have a responsibility to leave it safe for future generations. Give back now so the children of tomorrow do not have to pay the price for your excess.

Sometimes I feel pulled in too many directions, but I must dedicate my energies to contributing my leadership skills in order to help solve at least one major problem.

DAY 301

---○---

"Laugh and the world laughs with you,
snore and you sleep alone."
MRS. PATRICK CAMPBELL

*A*re you known as someone fun to work with, or are you known as somewhat blustery? How are you dividing your fun time and your work time? Many people develop a clear delineation between when it is all right to have a good time and when it is time to be serious. That makes sense. There are times when you have to be serious. Too often, however, seriousness overwhelms when fun would be fine. This happens especially during deadlines, crises, and times of insecurity. Sounds like every day, doesn't it?

No one says you have to be constantly joking. You need to be aware, however, of the need for a little levity, especially during times of high stress. Laughter decreases stress and makes people healthier and more productive. Find more fun time. Create and participate fully in a laughter-friendly environment.

The more stressful the work environment becomes, the more
important it is for me to allow for humor. Today I will take
action to be sure that our environment is laughter friendly.

DAY
302

---○---

*"The crocodile doesn't harm the bird that cleans his teeth
for him. He eats the others but not that one."*
LINDA HOGAN

There are people on the periphery of our daily lives who provide valuable services to us. Who are those people in your life? Just as in nature when creatures are involved in symbiotic relationships, all possible steps also must be taken to protect that relationship. Finding new people to take care of us as well as those already doing so is too costly.

Make a note of all the people upon whom you rely. Just as you expect their loyalty in helping you achieve your vision, they also have the right to expect the same loyalty from you. Do everything you can to protect them from attack Stand behind them. Give them the nourishment they need. Praise them. Honor them. Revere them. Find out their goals and do what you can to help them achieve them. They take care of you. You have a responsibility to take care of them.

*There are dozens of people who take care of me and symbiotically
work to help me achieve my dreams. I continually look for ways
to provide them the same protection that they provide to me.*

DAY
303

---○---

"Energy is the power that drives every human being.
It is not lost by exertion but maintained by it,
for it is a faculty of the psyche."
GERMAINE GREER

*E*nergy is a funny thing. We seem to have an overabundance of it at times, and then at other times we can hardly function. It is the driving force behind our accomplishments. If we do not have enough energy, or if those who are working with us do not have enough, we can never achieve our goals.

There is a correlation between the amount of energy that one has and the excitement one feels about a project. The more you like to do a certain activity, the more likely it is that you will have an excess of energy in conjunction with it.

You can do two things. First, start to see the tedious tasks as fun and exciting opportunities that help you reach your goals. Just a slight change in focus will assure you more energy. Second, be sure you are on the path you have chosen because it pleases you, not because it pleases someone else. If you are not excited about your vision, you will never excite others. Your excitement will draw an abundance of energy into any opportunity.

I strive to see all activities I undertake as opportunities that help me
reach my goals, and thus I enjoy an abundance of energy.

DAY 304

---

*O*nce you reach a certain level where things become comfortable and easy, there is a great temptation to stay there. Economic comfort increases the desire. We talk about people reaching the pinnacle of success in their lives, yet true success comes not from realizing a peak as much as initiating and making the journey.

The happiest people seem to be those who are constantly growing. They remain interested in developing their abilities, their careers, and their families. They do not remain static. Instead life is an ongoing process that unfolds as a flower, slowly and colorfully.

Choose where you are going. Keep moving. Keep developing. Dedicate yourself to worthy lifework. You will find that happiness and contentment stay as long as you are moving toward something notable.

My joy comes not from arriving at success but from the journey and the direction I take. Today I will examine myself for areas in which I have become static, and I will begin movement again.

DAY
305

---○---

"Revolutions never go backward."
RALPH WALDO EMERSON

*W*e are in a revolution. Major changes are taking place around the world that have an enormous effect on our lives. Human awareness is reaching an all-time high. People everywhere are gaining an understanding of issues that they never thought of before. Ecology, human rights, empowerment in the workplace, civil rights, the unacceptability of government corruption, human potential, crime, disease, and morality are issues on the forefront of the global consciousness.

This trend will not reverse itself. Direct your vision in a socially conscious manner. It is demanded of you. Leaders are held accountable now more than ever before. Higher demands are being placed on you each day. Accept the challenge. Lead with conscience. Lead with soul. Your values are needed and demanded more than ever before.

I have an enormous responsibility to move in a socially conscious manner. I am accountable for my actions in ways never before experienced and accept the challenge with an open and willing heart.

DAY 306

---○---

*I*t is human nature to repeat what we learn from authority
figures in our lives. Parents start the cycle by dem-
onstrating a set of values and a morality that many sons and
daughters carry unquestioningly throughout their lives. As long
as these values are healthy, it makes sense to continue the cycle.
Yet when unhealthy things are taught, the intelligent adult aban-
dons the practice and breaks the cycle.

Habits and values that we have learned from other leaders in
our lives are also repeated. Intelligent leaders look closely at the
values and practices they learned from others. They examine the
merit of upholding the behaviors acquired through exposure to
other leaders.

Never allow yourself to repeat a damaging cycle of behavior.
Unlike a family, your associates are not tied to you through the
bond of blood. They are tied only through your charisma and
your ability to motivate them. Motivate them with love and care
for their well-being.

*Today I will make a point to study my own leadership style and
question behaviors that I learned from past leaders and mentors.
I will determine whether or not I perpetuate what I learned.*

DAY
307

"Success has become a lobotomy to my past."
NORMAN MAILER

*H*undreds, perhaps thousands, have contributed to the successes you have experienced. Throughout your life people have made their marks on your personality, your style, your values, and your beliefs.

Never forget those who have helped you along the way. As your responsibilities grow, it is easy to lose touch with many of the most important people in your life. It is natural, too, for as you grow you sometimes outgrow those who helped. That is no excuse for forgetting, however.

Find ways to demonstrate your appreciation. Thank your family. Send a letter to an old college professor whose insights set you in the right direction. Make a phone call to a friend you miss. These small gestures will have tremendous meaning to the people who have supported you. They will also keep you in touch with the past, which has been so important in forming the present you now live.

The people who have helped me along my path deserve my gratitude.
Today I will take action to show my appreciation to someone
who has had an impact on my success.

DAY
308

"Mr. Morgan buys his partners; I grow my own."
ANDREW CARNEGIE

*E*ffective leaders surround themselves with loyal people. The people whom you lead must be loyal so that they can assist in accomplishing your vision. They can help you reach your objectives in countless ways, or they can snuff out your growth in an instant. Your support structure, family, friends, and colleagues need to know where you are going. Without their support you can never progress.

You can assure the loyalty of others by doing one thing: Return the loyalty. Let those whom you rely on know that you will be there for them when they need you. You will support their growth and development in the same way you expect them to support you. Ask them their goals. Find out their vision. Never forget that they are there for you as long as you are there for them. Loyalty is not generated by money alone. True loyalty comes from supporting the spirit and soul of those upon whom you depend.

I achieve my own growth through the loyalty of people at every level of my life. I honor them with the same degree of loyalty that I hope to receive.

DAY 309

---○---

"A leader who doesn't hesitate before he sends his nation into battle is not fit to be a leader."

GOLDA MEIR

One of the most crippling things in any organization is for its leaders to wait too long to make decisions. The competition senses when you are fearful or too bureaucratic to make timely decisions, and they take full advantage.

You are likely feeling more pressure than ever to make speedy decisions on every issue. The more you hesitate, the more opportunities you lose. Be careful, however, of making decisions without adequately calculating the cost and the risk. You can never have enough information, but do not let that stop you from examining the data at your disposal before jumping. Use your judgment skills. Be able to justify why you made a decision. You walk the tightrope between inaction and hyper-action. Fight the pressure when necessary. Much could be at risk.

I am a decisive leader. I will not lose sight, however, of the importance of calculating the costs and risks of the alternatives before taking action.

DAY 310

"Power can be taken, but not given. The process of the taking is empowerment in itself."
GLORIA STEINEM

No one is going to give you power. They may elevate you to a certain position in your organization. They may give you a title. They may provide you the opportunity and the forum to develop power. All of that is meaningless, however, unless you do something with what you have been provided. The world is full of impotent people with grand titles.

At the same time, the world is full of people with no title and no formal position who have become very powerful. The little person can move mountains with enough courage to speak up for his or her beliefs. Power is yours to take. You will only have it if you want it and are not afraid of it. Be secure. Be willing to take risks. Be willing to put your life and soul on the line for your beliefs. With strength, vision, and courage you will have more influence than you ever dreamed.

I readily embrace power in order to lead myself and others toward my vision.

DAY 311

---○---

*"Keep on going, and the chances are that you will
stumble on something, perhaps when you are least
expecting it. I never heard of anyone ever
stumbling on something sitting down."*
CHARLES F. KETTERING

*T*he road to your goals has most likely been long and
grueling. There are many obstacles along the way.
They often seem larger the closer we get to the achievement of
our vision. People sometimes just decide to sit down and accept
where they are rather than continue along a difficult and tenuous
path.

The hard part about obstacles is that sometimes they prevent
us from seeing what is beyond them. We sometimes forget that
between the obstacles there is a straight path that leads us to our
dreams. The only way to realize your dreams is to fearlessly continue on past the obstacles. Have the courage to get up and move
again when you trip and fall. Have faith in the road you choose
and in the beauty that lies just beyond the obstacles.

*The strength of my vision and my personal courage allows me
to overcome any obstacle that gets in my way.*

DAY
312

---○---

"A little rebellion now and then is a good thing."
THOMAS JEFFERSON

*L*eaders have to have strong egos in order to persuade others to follow along with them. Sometimes a strong ego can get in the way of listening to the discreet signals that others give us as they try to communicate that we are off purpose.

Ego often blinds us to the needs and desires of others. We can be unintentionally unfair. We can get so consumed in our work that our family suffers. When this happens, be prepared for a knock in the head. When you are not listening to the small cues, which will happen, sometimes the troops will use stronger methods. Take note. Accept rebellion as a fact of life. Deal with it when it occurs. Do not punish, but listen. It carries an important message. Your survival may depend on it. People do not rebel unless they care. Listen and accept their caring, and change when necessary to protect the overall vision.

When I become so obsessed that I no longer notice the discreet signals
of underlying trouble or tension, I may be forced to deal with
a stronger message. I listen and accept my part in any
rebellion and change when necessary to protect my vision.

DAY 313

---○---

"You must live in the present, launch yourself on every
wave, find your eternity in each moment."
HENRY DAVID THOREAU

*E*ven though the lifeblood of a leader is vision, it is not
the only sustaining force. People who live only for
goals, never taking their eyes off the road for a minute, lose the
beauty that surrounds them at every step. If you know where
you are going, but you do not fully appreciate where you are at
the moment, you may end up someplace that you do not want
to be.

Your children and your family are present with you on your
journey. Look at them and enjoy them while you have them. If
they do not know you while you are on the path toward your
dreams, they will not want to know you when you get there.
Although you can plan for your future, you can never plan on
the random events that could change your life. Who knows if
you will live to see the full completion of your dreams? As long
as you live while you are moving toward them, it will not matter
what tomorrow brings. Pay attention to the little things. Enjoy
the journey. The fun is in the going, not in the arrival.

Today I will find ways to stop along the journey to my dreams
and enjoy myself and those around me.

DAY 314

---○---

"People see God every day, they just don't recognize him."
PEARL BAILEY .

*T*here is more to the world than meets the eye. You may achieve a great deal of power as a leader. You have significant control over people, events, and organizations. You grow and develop in ways you never dreamed. You have a vision. You are on a quest. The world revolves around you and your dreams. You feel omnipotent.

When things are going well it is easy to lose sight of your spirituality. People tend to think of the God force in their lives when things are bad. Then they ask for help. Good things happen too. The smile of a small child or of a friend. The twinkle in their eyes that shows you a bit of their souls. The coincidence that comes along just when you are at the end of your rope. The beauty of nature. The energy of cities. The feeling inside of something more. Pay attention to these things. They guide you. They nourish you. They help to make all the effort worthwhile.

As I move along my journey, controlling many of the people and events that are in my life, I remember to keep in touch with my spirituality.

DAY 315

*"It is better to be part of a great whole than
to be the whole of a small part."*
FREDERICK DOUGLASS

*H*ave you been thinking big enough lately?

You have the ability to make a contribution in ways you may not have dreamed possible. You may not be able to conquer all the problems in the world, but your particular skills and vision can be a part of the cure to many of society's ills.

Small thinking can feel good because the feeling of success and accomplishment comes quickly and easily. If your goals are small and your dreams are self-serving, you will progress at a rapid rate. But to what? In the end you will ask yourself if it was all worth the effort. If you have not assisted in the grand scheme, you will feel like a small cog, important yet somehow capable of doing more. Dedicate yourself to something bigger. Give of your talents freely to create a future that you are proud to participate in; a future that you can leave as a legacy to future generations who need all the help they can get.

*There is a greater purpose in my life, and I have the talents and
skills to become part of something big. Today I will take action
to contribute on a grander scale than I previously dreamed.*

DAY 316

---

*T*here are a million reasons why your plans will not work. Any number of variables are working against you at any time. It is amazing that anyone can accomplish anything. One reason why successful people are able to realize so many of their dreams is that they refuse to take ownership of all the negativity that surrounds them.

The minute you say you cannot do something, you take ownership of your belief. Subconsciously you will do everything possible to assure that you are unable to do it. This holds true for any limitation you attempt to justify. It is normal to doubt. It becomes disabling when your doubts manifest themselves into realities, sabotaging your progress. Listen for the next time you find yourself using words like *can't, shouldn't, impossible,* and *unable.* Think of the implications. Then make a conscious effort to stop arguing for your limitations and to start arguing for your possibilities.

*When my doubts turn into justifications for my limitations,
I cause them to become real. Today I will focus on
consciously arguing for my possibilities.*

DAY 317

"*My only concern was to get home
after a hard day's work.*"

ROSA PARKS

Sometimes the simplest of motives can start an avalanche of change. You may have the grandest of all visions. That does not mean that your motives have to be as grand. Your motive may be as simple as wanting a better life for your children. You may want to find intellectual stimulation. You may just want to get home.

Whatever your vision, keep the motive in mind. The motive is the glue that holds your vision together. It is the compelling force that allows you to commit to the trials and difficulties of the journey. When you know why you are working on your dream, you can do almost anything to make it happen. You can make grand things happen. Recognize your basic motive and hold it in your mind to fortify your spirit.

*Today I will think about and clarify the reasons why I press forward
so diligently with my dream. The reasons give me the strength
to carry forth my compelling, long-term vision.*

DAY 318

"Experience is not what happens to you, it's what you do with what happens to you."
ALDOUS HUXLEY

The soul of life is both dark and light. No matter how hard we try or how much we pray, bad things happen. Nobody likes it, but just as life provides joy and beauty, the pendulum swings to sorrow and ugliness. We cannot stop life from happening. We cannot stop the bad and only have good. The only thing we can control is the way we view the dark side of our lives.

Perhaps it is true that the only way we can learn to appreciate ecstasy is through the experience of suffering. Without suffering there would be no context for pleasure. If that were all that suffering gave us, it would be enough. When you suffer through bad experiences, you have a choice. You can weep about the pain, or you can choose to learn from it. You can use it as a context for understanding yourself and your experiences. Life will hand you both good and bad. Rejoice in the good. Savor the bad for what it can teach you.

I choose to accept light and dark as inevitable, each with its purpose to teach me and help me grow.

DAY 319

"Love not what you are but only what you may become."
MIGUEL DE CERVANTES

*T*hat moment when you become satisfied with yourself and your current situation you lose all your power. When you live only in the present, dealing only with the now, you become stagnant. With so much business in your life, you may find it tempting to focus on the immediate. Why worry about tomorrow when there is so much taking up your time today?

Focusing on the immediate is not the same as focusing on the important. The immediate usually takes away from the important. What important areas of your future and the future of your organization and community are you neglecting because you are so entrenched in the business of the day? Do not be proud because you finished your daily checklist and managed to put out a few fires too. Be proud when you can dedicate energy to the important issues you face as well as keeping up with the present. Only then can you know what you are able to become. Only then will you feel energized about your life in all its possibilities.

I fight any temptation to dedicate all my energy to the immediate problems of the day. I handle the immediate issues only in the context of the important.

DAY 320

---○---

*L*eaders everywhere are embracing a new style. It is a style based on cooperation and collaboration. The surprise is that even though the people who used to be called subordinates griped because no one ever listened to them, now that they are called associates they gripe because they are accountable.

Leaders must be sure they are developing systems that reward those who participate freely in the decision-making process and accept accountability. If you ask people to accept more risk, it is only reasonable that you find ways to compensate that risk and reward the kind of behavior that will bring growth. Feel free to ask more of others, but be willing to give more in return for their willingness to play the game by the new rules.

Today I will make sure that I am rewarding the kind of behaviors that will help reinforce the new leadership style that relies on the cooperation and collaboration of everyone involved in the goals.

DAY 321

---○---

"Blessed is the influence of one true, loving
human soul on another."
GEORGE ELIOT

*C*hances are there have been several influential people
in your life who have guided you, directed you, and
found ways to open doors and opportunities that you could never
have found on your own. These mentors have made an indelible
impact on your life. As you continue along your path, other
mentors will be there to clear the way and make your journey
smoother.

Your mentors have done this because they too have been men-
tored. It is a tradition as old as leadership itself. Just as others
have chosen to mentor you, you also must choose to mentor
others. When you run across others willing to ask for your help,
extend it to them freely. When you see others with potential
who just need a little boost, give it to them. Keep the tradition
fresh and alive. When you help someone else, a little bit of your
soul lives through that person and continues as he or she passes
on your wisdom and charity to others who need help in the
future.

I readily help others who need my guidance and support
to further their dreams and bolster their souls.

DAY 322

Come to the edge.
No. We will fall.

Come to the edge.
No. We will fall.

They came to the edge
and they flew.

G. APOLLINAIRE

*L*eadership is about learning to use faith as the wings that hold you up as you glide over the possibilities, soar over your vision, and land softly and securely where others only dream.

Your courage will help others fly just as you do. If you have a vision and the passionate commitment to see it through, your excitement will move others closer to the edge. Your customers will follow you. Your team members will go together with you. Your leaders will take the leap of faith when they see that you, too, are willing to leap along with them. You have the dream. Be sure that you have the courage to do what it takes to see the dream come true.

Today I will take a courageous step that I have been putting off
but that will help me move closer to my vision.

DAY 323

When was the last time you sent a thank-you note or gift to your spouse? What about your children? Your boss? A team member who really pulled through at the last minute and kept you out of the hot seat? Your mentor? Your customers? Your favorite grammar school teacher? People do not show their appreciation enough in our culture.

People will do almost anything for you—once. If they do not feel appreciated, do not expect any more favors. However, if you display your gratitude lavishly and sincerely, you are guaranteed that people will do things for you over and over again. It may seem like a selfish way to look at it, but it is true that you need others to help you accomplish your goals. Those who help you deserve the respect of a formal thank you. Let them know how much their actions mean to you. Do it for yourself. But do it for them too; it means so much to hear it from you.

*Today I will write at least one past-due thank-you note.
I will speak lavishly of my gratitude because it means
so much for people to hear it from me.*

DAY 324

---○---

"To defend one's self against fear is simply to insure that one will, one day, be conquered by it; fears must be faced."
JAMES BALDWIN

*O*ne of the biggest fears that people face is confrontation. In most organizations people will go to extreme lengths to avoid discussing issues in conflict. The talk is polite but not sincere. People are often willing to discuss problems with everyone but the person with whom they are having the problem.

Communication is more important than ever because of the increasing interdependence among associates. By avoiding confrontation, you only prevent any collaboration because you never get the issues out on the table.

The rules for confrontation are simple. Keep the discussion objective. Do not judge. Express your sentiments in an exploring manner. Listen to hear what the other person is saying, not to plan your response.

Look together for mutually workable solutions. If you have conflicts, bring them to the forefront. Do not hide. They will not go away. Communication is fundamental to your survival.

I take action to successfully confront someone when conflict occurs and search together for mutually workable solutions.

DAY 325

"You can never give complete authority and over-all power to anyone until trust can be proven."

BILL COSBY

There is an emotional safety net that has to be in place in order for you to gain the trust of the individuals you lead. If they do not feel protected by their leader, they will find ways to provide self-protection.

Self-protection manifests itself in the form of withholding key information. You will see it in people's failure to open up and tell you what they really feel or what is really going on in the organization. If there is not an overall feeling of psychological safety, people will form alliances against each other. Whoever has the most powerful and influential alliance will have the most security.

Stop that cycle by assuring an environment of open communication and tolerance for mistakes. Be the protective layer that shields people from the negative forces they face from inside and outside of the organization.

I understand fully the importance of providing a psychologically safe environment for others. Today I will examine where I need to improve in this area, and take steps to do so.

DAY 326

*"To lift up a fallen man is good. To help him
lift himself up is better."*

FRANK TYGER

*H*ow can organizations and the people who work in
them become more socially responsible? The old
model of financial assistance through cash handouts does not
work. It ties people to a dependence. It causes a spiral of need
that never goes away because the recipients of the aid never learn
the necessary skills to get out of the trap.

Restructure the way you approach your philanthropic endeavors. Find ways to provide jobs and training to people who need
your help. Maybe your organization could use persons from a
homeless shelter or a sheltered workshop to assemble key product
components. Can you volunteer on the board of an organization
that trains people in new job skills? Your leadership would be
invaluable.

As government gets out of the welfare business, leaders in both
the profit and nonprofit sectors will have to be more inventive
and more selective in their giving in order to prevent more people
from falling through the cracks.

*Today I will take action to evaluate my strategy as a socially
responsible leader. There is a tremendous amount of need,
and I have much to offer.*

DAY 327

"There is no substitute for thorough-going, ardent, and sincere earnestness."

CHARLES DICKENS

When you study organizations that really grow and prosper, you find that the people in them have an extraordinary amount of enthusiasm. It permeates everything they do. People are selected for their eagerness to be there. Money is an issue, but not as much as desire. Experience takes a backseat to passion.

Leaders can learn from this model. Too often leaders believe that the right person for any position is the one with the most experience. That is fine only if they are enthusiastic and want to be with you. If they feel as if they are doing you a favor, they will not stay. Simple.

What keeps enthusiastic people in an organization? Visionary leaders who are enthusiastic. Your attitude is contagious. Your vision has to be tangible and compelling. Find earnest people. Provide them the support and encouragement they need. They will make you great and have a good time doing it.

I model enthusiasm and provide a compelling vision in order to perpetuate the passion I love to see in others.

327

DAY 328

---

*"To every disadvantage there is
a corresponding advantage."*
W. CLEMENT STONE

*L*ooking for the negative in every idea is a common tendency among people. It is our way of analyzing. We learn it in elementary school when we are taught about hypotheses. A hypothesis is an educated guess that is assumed correct until proven wrong. We do experiments to prove our theories are wrong. It manifests itself later in life when we hear a suggestion and answer with the words, "Yes, but . . ."

Few words are as damaging to the creative process as "Yes, but . . ." They immediately send any conversation into a downward spiral until most ideas are effectively killed. You can change your organizational culture and personal life by eliminating these words from your vocabulary and replacing them with "Yes, and . . ."

Find ways to look for the possibilities in any new concept. You will find more new opportunities when you are making an effort to look for them.

*Today I will encourage even more of an emphasis
on looking for possibilities without losing
the realism of looking at potential risks.*

DAY
329

---○---

*"The future belongs to those who believe
in the beauty of their dreams."*
ELEANOR ROOSEVELT

You do not have to be told about the effectiveness of having a dream and believing in it enough to make it come true. Your dreams are the foundations upon which every other thing you do as a leader rests. Believing in them is the first step to taking the action you need to accomplish them.

What about the other people in your network? They have dreams too. Do they believe in them, or do they just consider them fancies? Do they believe in your dreams? Focus some of your effort on finding out the dreams of the people whom you depend on. Encourage them to believe in their dreams and to take action on them. Align them with yours. Work together.

You need others to help you achieve your dreams. They need you to teach them how to believe in their own dreams and to show them how to make them come true.

*I deeply believe in my own dreams and today will work with someone
else to help them believe in the beauty of their dreams.*

DAY 330

---

*"I do the very best I know how—the very best I can;
and I mean to keep doing so until the end."*
ABRAHAM LINCOLN

There will be times when all your best efforts will fail. You will probably hold out longer than you should hoping that a miracle will happen to turn things around. It could be that the project grows too far outside of your expertise. It could be that external factors prevent success. It could be bad timing. Perhaps it is just not meant to be.

Whatever the reason for disappointment, never let it be because you did not try hard enough. Few things are worse for your reputation and sense of self-worth than not to have done the best job you possibly could given the circumstances and tools available. No one can ask for more, yet people have every right to demand just that. At the same time, know when you have done your best and it is time to release. You will drive yourself crazy trying to make something work that cannot be done. Your talents are too valuable to waste on hopeless tasks.

*On any project or activity, I dedicate myself to doing the best that
I can. No one expects any more or any less from me.*

DAY 331

---○---

*"To be a success in business, be daring,
be first, be different."*
HENRY MARCHANT

What are you doing to differentiate yourself from all the others? This question relates to you as well as to your product, service, or organization. It is a basic question that leaders must constantly ask of themselves. The world has become hyper-competitive. Technology has made it possible to copy almost any new idea in a short time.

Your differentiation strategy is the key to remaining competitive. You will find your difference in levels of price, quality, and delivery. You and your product must be perceived as a good value. Be innovative. Take risks. It does you no good to copy someone else. If they were first, they have the advantage. Instead, find a new way to approach an old problem. Find a new service that you can offer. Find new ways to add value that distinguishes you from all others.

*The way I differentiate myself, my products, my services,
and my organization is the key to competitive success.
Today I will examine in what ways I can add
more value in new and unique ways.*

DAY 332

---○---

"The strongest principle of growth lies in human choice."
GEORGE ELIOT

The only way for you to access your potential is to make choices. Every action you take involves making a choice. Will you turn right or left at a street light? The phone is ringing. Will you answer it immediately? Will you say hello to someone you pass in the hallway?

No one has trouble with the automatic choices made on seemingly innocuous issues, yet each choice propels you in a new direction, opening or closing new potentials. When there is too much information or when the risk appears to be high, choices become difficult. Not knowing what will happen when we make a choice can stop us from choosing the potential with the most reward. The irony is that the simple act of not choosing is a choice that opens up a potential that may not be as desirable. If you are holding back on taking action that could be rewarding, make the choice. Then steer into it. The possibilities await only after you open up the potential.

Only in making choices can I open up the potential that awaits me.
Today I will choose to take action on something that
I have been putting off for too long.

DAY 333

*"Concern should drive us into action
and not into a depression."*
KAREN HORNEY

We are exposed on a daily basis to an astonishing amount of distressing news. The economy is in a tailspin. The world situation is chaotic. Children are starving everywhere. There is war where there should be peace. There are homeless people who should have places to live. The rain forest is being depleted. The earth is warming, and the ice caps are melting.

It is enough to send anyone into a depression. Going into a depressed state, however, is not going to help things get better. Action helps things get better. Action alleviates anxiety. Focus on what you can do. Nothing is hopeless. Every social ill can be treated. One dedicated person can make a difference. As a leader, you can make more of a difference by using your influencing skills to motivate others to take action. Your example and contribution can make the difference and turn the tide on an injustice or danger.

*I have the ability to make a difference and turn the tide
on an injustice or danger, and today I will take action
on an issue that is important to me.*

DAY
334

—○—

"Patience is bitter, but its fruit is sweet."
LIDA CLARKSON

*L*eaders are ambitious by nature. Most have a tremendous amount of things that they want to accomplish in their lives. Along with their sense of ambition comes a sense of urgency. They basically want things to happen when they want them to happen, and forget the natural progression of events.

One of the hardest virtues for leaders to learn is patience. It is not part of their typical personality profile. That does not mean that leaders cannot be patient. It means that they have to practice and use logic to overcome their innate desires. When you are feeling impatient, ask yourself if it is part of your nature or if you have a true reason. Chances are you have to learn to relax and let things run their course. You may be able to set things into motion, but the natural laws of the universe are going to set the time frame for them to come to fruition. Practice patience. When the time is right, you will know, and it will be worth the wait.

It is natural that I feel impatient, but I expertly avoid rushing things along faster than their natural course.

DAY 335

"*The fullness of life is in the hazards of life. And, at the worst, there is that in us which can turn defeat into victory.*"

EDITH HAMILTON

*S*ome people like risk more than do others. That is not a surprise. Perhaps they just learned that along with the fear that one feels doing something risky, there is a sense of life and invigoration. Take skiing. It requires courage to stand on top of a mountain and push off, especially when you are first learning. You feel out of control. You feel helpless. Yet at the same time there is the wonderful feeling of the wind blowing against your face as you speed down a mountain. Adrenaline pumps. The exceptional beauty of the outdoors surrounds you.

The next time you are in a risky situation and begin to feel overcome by doubts and fears, remember that it is hardest just before the jump. After that you can focus on the exhilaration. It will still be scary, but you are in motion. You are taking action toward a sense of freedom and accomplishment.

When I am about to undertake something risky I focus on the exhilaration of the adventure and the feeling of accomplishment I will feel as an outcome of my decision.

DAY
336

---○---

"Judge a man by his questions rather than his answers."
VOLTAIRE

*A*s a leader you are surely asked by others for your opinions and your advice. It is flattering. It shows that you are respected for your experience and ideas. What do you do when you need advice? It is not easy to find good counselors. It is easy to find people who will give you advice, however.

The key thing to look for in an advisor is not his or her opinion. If someone offers an opinion too readily, be suspicious. Look for someone who asks you questions first. Someone with experience wants to be sure to give you the recommendations that will fit your situation. They cannot know your situation by just observing you. They need to understand the history of your condition, what your motives are, and what you desire as an outcome. That can only come through interrogation. When people ask you questions, answer them openly. Be honest. That is the only way the advice will be valid. Then hold on to that person as a trusted counselor. Good advice is hard to find.

When I need advice, I readily go in search of it and find it in people who are willing to take the time to listen to and understand my situation first.

DAY 337

---○---

"If you wish your merit to be known, acknowledge that of other people."

ASIAN PROVERB

You can never give the people around you enough praise. Most people want to be noticed for their accomplishments more than anything else. This need begins in childhood. Universally, when children are engaged in any activity where they are mastering a task, they turn around to be sure someone is watching. "Mommy, look!" That is one of the first sentences most children learn.

We do not give up that need when we grow up. Adults crave recognition as much as children. A leader who realizes that will find ways to acknowledge others. They give others credit for the work they perform effectively. Good leaders never take credit for someone else's effort. They do not need to. The people you acknowledge will be so pleased with your recognition that they will sing your praises too. Find ways to praise. Anyone. Everyone. They crave it. You can satisfy their hunger.

Today I will make it a point to acknowledge someone deserving whom I may not have noticed much before.

DAY 338

When you have a new plan or idea there are all sorts of things that can and will go wrong. Ask your banker, and she or he will give you a hundred reasons why your start-up will not work. Look at the economic picture, and you will find undeniable data that things are getting worse than ever. Listen to the politicians during an election, and you will be convinced that the country is in such bad shape that it is hardly worth living in anymore.

They are all right. When you are staring bad news in the face it is impossible to ignore. That does not mean, however, that you have to accept it. With the right attitude you can be successful regardless of any reality. Scientifically a bumblebee cannot fly. Try telling that to a bumblebee that flies in the face of reality every day. If you believe and have evidence to prove you are right, you have a good chance of leapfrogging over the negative truth. Like the bumblebee, deny it, but then flap your wings like crazy. And never stop once you are airborne.

*I take advisors and general indicators seriously, but their indications
are not my only consideration. Like a bumblebee, I can deny
it all and fly if my idea and plan are good enough.*

DAY
339

---○---

"The graveyards are full of indispensable people."
CHARLES DE GAULLE

*I*n times of economic insecurity and downsizing, it becomes extremely difficult to get people to take the time off that they need to rest and recharge their batteries. Some fear that if they take time off it will become obvious that the organization can get along without them, which may land them next on the chopping block. Some people truly believe that things would not function without them and do not dare to take time off because of the mess they would find upon their return.

As the old saying goes, no one has ever lain on a deathbed and said, "I wish I had worked more." You are most effective when you are developing other people to be responsible on their own, without your constant supervision. You should be able to disappear. You should be able to think strategically. You should have time off. No matter how indispensable you believe you are, the organization will get on without you.

Be sure you are taking enough time away. Spend it with your family. They are there for only a little while. Spend it with yourself. You deserve the time to rest and think. The organization will be there when you get back.

I will act today to plan some time away in order to recharge myself and renew my personal relationships.

DAY 340

---

*"We live in a wonderful world that is full of beauty,
charm, and adventure. There is no end to
the adventures that we can have if only
we seek them with our eyes open."*
JAWAHARLAL NEHRU

When was the last time you felt as if you had been on an adventurous journey? Most people believe that adventures are to be experienced sparingly. We save them for a vacation. We allow ourselves a few days a year to be daring, to do something different that leaves us awestruck.

Adventures can be experienced every day. It all depends on your attitude. You are surrounded by new stimuli, so get out of your daily rut and look around. Starting a conversation with someone you never met can be adventurous. An adventure can be as simple as trying a new ethnic food. You could take a different route to work and discover a new part of your town. You could take a class. You could plan a trip to somewhere you have always considered exotic.

Life is more exciting when it is varied. There is so much to see and experience. Get out of your rut and try something new. The perspective will open your senses and keep you fresh.

*Today I will do something different and discover new ways
to heighten my sense of adventure.*

DAY 341

*"Both tears and sweat are salty, but they render
a different result. Tears will get you sympathy,
sweat will get you change."*

JESSE JACKSON

*T*oo often our days are filled with complaints. People complain to us. We complain to ourselves. We complain to others. It is easy to fall into the trap of joining the BMW Club, which stands for the Blamers, Moaners, and Whiners. Do you know anyone in that club? You probably know a few vested, lifetime members.

Do not fall into the BMW trap. It is easy to do. Leaders attend a seemingly endless string of meetings. Many fall into discussion sessions where problems are aired at length, with no action taken. Complaining is the most unproductive of activities if it stops there. You can blame, moan, and whine all you want, but you will never feel better until you take action to resolve the problem. Take action. It *is* work. It is sometimes painful. At the same time, action is constructive and is often the only way to bring about change to end the things that are causing you all the pain and grief.

*I make a point to take action on issues where I have a complaint.
My courage inspires others to stop blaming, moaning,
and whining and start winning instead.*

DAY 342

"It really takes guts to take a stand."
SHIRLEY CHISHOLM

*T*he world is full of injustice. There is no denying it. In the workplace leaders sometimes feel pressure to compromise their values and beliefs for fear of losing their jobs or to receive promotions.

When you are right, you should take a stand. Act courageously, even though pain might be involved. The people who make the greatest contributions to our society are the ones with the fortitude to stand up for right. When they see injustice, they do something about it. They maintain integrity by standing by their values.

Stand by your values. Make your contribution to our society, even on a small level. Your strength gives others the strength to pick up where you left off and carry on to a more just world and workplace.

I am a courageous leader, admired for my willingness to take a stand on the tough issues. I do not hesitate to make my position clear when I feel pressured to compromise my values.

DAY 343

What do you most need to be an effective leader? You could probably fill a page with the list of your needs; the cooperation of others would be a good start. Perhaps clear vision from your leaders. Maybe advice and guidance from a mentor. Perhaps you need more support from your family. Maybe you want your team to push just a little harder. A day off to rest. More money. The list goes on and on.

No one can read your mind, yet one of the hardest challenges leaders face is asking for something. Instead we try to make our needs implicitly clear, sending out signals and hoping people will read them. Make your needs explicit. When you want something, ask. The people in your life want you to be successful, and they want to be successful themselves. If you let them know how you both can be successful, and what you need in the process, they will help you get it. Communicate what you want and justify the need. The world is yours for the asking.

*I recognize the importance of making my needs clear if I want
to satisfy them. Today I will make it a point
to clearly ask for what I need.*

DAY
344

---○---

"For the purposes of action, nothing is more useful than narrowness of thought combined with energy of will."
HENRI FREDERIC AMIEL

A key precept for leaders is that they must take action. Without taking action you will be ineffective and impotent. Yet taking action alone is not enough. Along with action, you must have clear goals and direction. Your vision has to be broad enough to encompass all the opportunity available to you, yet it also must be narrow and focused.

When your focus is narrow it is easiest for you to generate the energy needed to make things happen. Lasers exhibit the power of narrow focus. A car headlight is like an unfocused laser beam. The energy present can spread a band of light for a distance of about fifty feet. If you take the same energy and focus it into a narrow beam, the power becomes so intense that it could burn a hole in a tree from a distance of two miles.

Focus your vision as narrowly as possible. The resulting energy will give you a burning power. The action you take will be clear and directed. Your accomplishments will be supercharged.

Today I will review my vision and goals to assure that I maintain a continuous and powerful laser-beam focus.

DAY 345

---

*"It is the creative potential itself in human beings
that is the image of God."*

MARY DALY

*T*he ability to dream an idea and then set about to create it is one of the principal things that sets us apart from all other life forms on earth. It is a tremendous gift. Every human being has the potential to create, which carries responsibility with it, especially for leaders. Not only do we have the drive to create something from our dreams, but we also have the responsibility to encourage and enable the same in others.

As with any gift, people are meant to use their creative abilities to make dreams happen. Your task is to nurture that belief in yourself and others. You demonstrate the potential.

Through the ability to create, everyone is like God. Creating something from nothing is a great power. It is a power strong enough to move the world. Do your part to move the world. Help others do their part too. In this way, you can re-create the world every day, each creation making it just a little bit better than before.

*I openly act upon my own gift of creativity and encourage everyone
I lead to create reality from their dreams and
contribute positively to the world.*

DAY 346

---

*"In life, as in a football game, the principle
to follow is: Hit the line hard."*
THEODORE ROOSEVELT

*S*low, *cautious,* and *incremental* used to be the buzzwords
describing change for leaders. There are advantages to
incremental change in an organization. It is easy to manage. It is
measurable. If you make a mistake, you can stop whatever it is
that you are doing without much damage. People are comfortable
with it because it is easier to adapt to slow change than to fast
change.

Be wary of being too cautious when you implement change
programs. The problems you and your organization face are coming at shock speed. A slow, tenuous reaction may be just as
detrimental as doing nothing.

React appropriately to the changes being faced. Radical change
in pace with the work environment may be the most appropriate
measure. It may carry more of a toll on people with it, but it
may also assure your survival and prosperity. Move fast when
necessary. Move hard. If your survival is at stake, the "revolution-
ary" approach may save your life.

*Today I will examine areas where we may be moving too slowly and
take appropriate action to assure our survival and prosperity.*

DAY 347

"Real joy comes not from ease or riches or the praise of men, but from doing something worthwhile."
W. T. GRANFELL

*W*hen your life draws to an end, you will not judge yourself by the amount of money you made. You will not care much about the specific deals you made or the political battles that you won. Your thoughts, instead, will turn to a review of your worthy accomplishments.

Measure everything you do against the worthiness of the purpose. Who are you helping? What contribution are you making to the world? What messages are you sending to your children or those who look to you for guidance? You work hard. You expend a tremendous amount of energy in your day-to-day life. There has to be a reason for it. In your twilight years you will want to be able to look back with pride, knowing that your presence in the world made a contribution in some small way to the betterment of humankind.

My efforts are worthwhile when I am dedicated to a worthy purpose. Today I will examine my direction and make sure I am headed on a course that I will always be proud of.

DAY 348

*"Men are wise in proportion, not to their experience,
but to their capacity for experience."*
GEORGE BERNARD SHAW

*E*very leader confronts the prospect of responding to people with fresh faces, who have no qualifications but who ask for a chance to prove their worth. You listen to their stories, and your heart goes out to them. Periodically you regret that you need someone with experience when you feel that someone without it deserves a chance. That person has not had a break. You could make the difference in a life.

Experience does not guarantee quality. Experience only gives you an idea of someone's education. Enthusiasm and aptitude are greater indicators of potential. When you are faced with these situations, remember that you hold an enormous amount of power. You really could be the factor that propels that special person toward success. Give people a chance whenever you can. If the eagerness and ability are there, experience cannot be far behind.

*I have a great opportunity to make a difference in someone's life
who otherwise might never have the opportunity to succeed
I do everything I can to help the worthy triumph*

DAY 349

"FEAR is nothing more than False Evidence Appearing Real."

ZIG ZIGLAR

*W*orry has to be one of the key cripplers of humankind. While some amount of worrying is good because it keeps us alert and helps us watch out for potential danger, it is seldom that worry should be considered anything other than dangerous in itself.

Mulling possibilities of everything bad that can happen will never help a situation. Actually, the bad scenarios invented by worry are false because they have never occurred. The mind invents possibilities. The whole process converts to fear and fearful behavior.

The next time you find yourself overcome with worry, ask yourself if you are doing all you can to prevent your fears from becoming real. If you are, then shut the worry away. There is nothing more you can do. Occupy yourself with productive activity. You will find that most of the fears generated by worry never come true.

When overwhelmed by worry, I find productive activity to keep me occupied and to stop the false inventions of my mind from crippling me.

DAY
350

---○---

*"Apparent failure may hold in its rough shell the germs
of a success that will blossom in time, and bear
fruit throughout eternity."*
FRANCES ELLEN WATKINS HARPER

*A*s leaders we make a tremendous number of plans. They function like maps, guiding us on our journey, helping us find our way in a quest toward our vision. Maps are not always accurate however. When the early European explorers set off to find new lands their maps only displayed the world as it was known then. We can laugh at their inaccuracies now and marvel at the fact that they were even able to use them as guides.

Your personal maps are the same. They only show the world as you know it. Even though your plan seems accurate, it will not always get you where you want to go. When that happens, rather than lamenting the failure, realize that as long as you are still remaining on purpose, you can find other ways to get there. As the explorers did, you too will eventually find treasure at the end of your journey.

*I often review my plans in order to steer away from hurdles,
so that I am always sailing toward my vision, regardless
of any minor failure along the way.*

DAY 351

"He conquers who endures."
ITALIAN PROVERB

Sometimes it seems as though you will never get the big break that you need to really come close to achieving your goals. You try and try. You talk to all the right people. You work hard. You courageously move toward your goals without fear and apprehension. You fight to win. You have ambition. You have drive. Yet nothing happens!

Perseverance is the factor that finally brings you over the edge. Unfortunately, many people give up on their goals or compromise on them, because they do not have patience. It is hard to hold your enthusiasm when there is a new obstacle around every corner. You have to, however. You have a vision that is strong and sound. Be patient. It may take only one more phone call. You may need only one more day or one more week. Keep your eye on the end result, and you will be able to persevere to make it happen.

Today I take action to be sure that I stick to my goals, no matter how restless I feel. Success is just around the corner.

DAY 352

---

*T*here are so many wonderful activities to waste time on. Television can be a great pacifier. Gossip can be so titillating. The game on the computer is so tempting. Just one more time, and you can beat your last score. The problem with these activities, and others like them, is that they rob your time. They are thieves of the most precious commodity you own.

Your time is limited. You cannot earn more. You cannot borrow more. You can only use it. Some people choose to spend it on meaningless activity. Some, instead, choose to invest it in their future. Each minute is so precious that you must use it wisely. If you have an idea, do it now. Do not wait. You just waste the time you have to make it happen. Seize the minute. This life is short, and there is so much good to do.

*I invest my time in activities that move me toward my vision.
Today I take special care to make sure I am
using time wisely and effectively.*

DAY 353

---○---

*"A kind heart is a fountain of gladness, making
everything in its vicinity freshen into smiles."*
WASHINGTON IRVING

What could you do to bring a smile to someone today? What little act of kindness would go a long way to making the sun shine in someone's eyes, even on a rainy day? People live guarded lives to protect themselves from the bad things. They long to be treated in some special way, even though they never expect it to happen.

You will bring joy to someone else and feel good about yourself if you find ways to be a little kinder. Do something special for someone. Maybe all you have to do is acknowledge their presence. Give someone a ride. Give them your seat when you do not have to. Buy a little present for someone you do not know. That little bit of compassion you show can make someone feel human again and remind them that the world is not impersonal and uncaring. You can demonstrate that it is full of hope, compassion, surprise, and adventure.

*Today I will do something special for someone. My kindness and
compassion may give them hope, as well as nourish my sense
of love and contribution to a greater purpose.*

DAY 354

*A*mong the temptations that leaders face, one of the
most destructive is the urge to surround ourselves
with people who mirror us. It is a natural tendency in our culture
to avoid confrontation. Leaders can accomplish that by assuring
that there is never anyone on the team who will confront. Instead, the team consists of friends and colleagues with the same
talents and interests.

Challenge yourself when you face the same temptation. Effective leaders surround themselves with people who complement
their talents. They reward those who disagree. You are responsible
to set the vision and lead the charge. Trust in those around you
to keep you focused on your own vision. Allow them to confront
you just as you reserve the right to confront them. Your leadership
will always be stronger as a result.

*I strive to surround myself with people who complement the talents
that I have and reward them for challenging me to stay focused.*

DAY 355

*E*ven when we are focused on our purpose and moving in the right direction, we sometimes go into automatic pilot. Monday comes and goes, and before we know it, Monday is back again. One week blends into another. It seems as though we could go through it all with our eyes closed.

It is dangerous to allow this to happen. You wake up one day feeling that you have lost months and disgusted because you do not feel any farther ahead. You may go on tenaciously working on your plan, and when you stop months later to take a breath, you realize you missed a major turn that you should have taken to send you off in the right direction. You then have to backtrack, losing precious moments in the meantime.

Review your plans regularly. Do not allow yourself to become caught up in the daily grind without taking a breather to be sure you want to be going where you are going. Stop once in a while and enjoy the journey. You will be happier, and you will be more likely to stay headed in the right direction.

I carefully watch myself to be sure that I take a breather once in a while, evaluate the direction I am headed, and enjoy the journey.

DAY
356

*"Sometimes we stare so long at a door that is closing
that we see too late the one that is open."*
ALEXANDER GRAHAM BELL

*S*tubbornness has been the downfall of many a leader. As controlling people, leaders feel that they can change the world with the sheer strength of their will. This is true in many cases. However, insisting on moving in one certain direction is not always the best idea.

Sharp leaders keep an eye out for opportunities at all times. They persistently pursue the vision they hold. Not all opportunities are created equally, however, and sometimes it is better to let something go when you realize it might not be the opportunity you originally thought it was. The more stubbornly you chase something that is not worth the effort, the more likely it will be that you will not see a better possibility cross your path. Constantly evaluate where you are. Choose your direction, but remember you do not have to stick with it if it is not taking you where you want to go.

*I critically appraise my direction at all times. Today I will explore
my options so that I am headed in the right direction, and if
I am not, I have the courage and foresight to change.*

DAY 357

---

*"Service is just a day-in, day-out, ongoing, never-ending,
unremitting, persevering, compassionate type of activity."*
LEON GORMAN

*I*f leaders are in any business, it is the service business.
It does not matter if your organization manufactures
automobiles or if you lead a troop of Boy Scouts. What matters
is remembering that you have a tremendous responsibility to
serve those who make it possible for you to live as a leader of
people.

You also serve your customers. Every leader has customers.
They are the people who pay your way, so to speak. They are
the distributors and the car buyers if you manufacture cars. They
are your team members. They are the parents of the members of
the church school class you teach or even the members themselves. Honor those you serve. Serve them with all your heart.
Without them your existence could never have the fulfillment
and meaning that it does.

*Today I will take steps to assure that I am serving the people
who sponsor my existence well, with passion and
comprehension of their needs.*

DAY
358

Your passion gives you the purpose of your being. With it you know where you have to go in order to fulfill your life. Passion alone will never get you anywhere until you do something with it. Action is key to everyone's success, whether or not they consider themselves leaders.

Having focused goals and a plan is necessary to be sure you head in the right direction to achieve your passion. Without goals and plans you will go nowhere. Sometimes people establish goals and plans, then sit back and wait for things to happen. Nothing does. You are the catalyst that makes things happen in your life. You are the match that sets your passions afire.

Live an action-oriented life. Encourage those you come into contact with to live a life of action. Fulfillment comes through living your passion, never through thinking and dreaming about it.

*I consciously work toward turning my passions into action. Today
I will review my goals and aspirations and take action in
at least one area where I need to and have not done so.*

DAY
359

---○---

*"Things turn out best for those who make the best
about the way things turn out."*
HUBERT HUMPHREY

Regardless of all the planning and action we take, life has a way of throwing us curve balls once in a while. We are only one force of nature, but through our plans we try to control the entire world around us. This is impossible. There are other forces of nature at work that add variables we could never have thought of and would never have wanted.

When life throws you a curve ball, remember that what you do with it is important. Nothing can be too bad if a lesson is learned. The biggest tragedy can be overcome if you find a way to make something positive come out of it. We are the most adaptable species on Earth. We can mold almost any set of circumstances to our viewpoint.

Remember the old saying the next time you face a situation that is less than pleasant: When life gives you lemons, make lemonade.

*I am most productive when I find ways to turn
bad situations into positive ones.*

DAY 360

*A*s the changes in our working and living environments begin to affect more people, you will see the need to adapt more clearly than most. You have access to more information. You have the leadership experience to know that things cannot remain the same. Other people you work with will resist too much change, especially if it affects their sense of security.

Stand firm in your decisions to move in new directions. You will feel a tremendous amount of pressure to stay where you are. You must forge new paths. Journeying in the same direction will often lead to diminishing returns. Insist on moving in other ways, sometimes completely opposite to the way you are accustomed. Your actions will open up opportunities that are as unimaginable as the future that is bringing the change.

I gladly accept the challenge to create and adapt to change. I am able to effectively motivate others to do the same.

DAY 361

"I can't work without a model."
VINCENT VAN GOGH

*L*eaders have many characteristics in common with artists. They can take an abstract concept seen only in their mind and turn it into a reality. They create new visions and help others to see them.

Like artists, leaders need models. They need to observe tangible representations of life, then combine and mold them into their own sense of what the world should be. Learn from other leaders. Model their style and adapt what you learn to grow your own. Unlike mentors, you do not need to know your models personally. You can read about them. You can frame their ideas with yours and create yourself, as you would create the world around you. Find models. Learn from them. Grow from them. Artists never stop using models. Leaders should not stop using them either.

Today I will make it a point to enrich my understanding of myself by finding excellent leadership models and emulating them in conjunction with my own style.

DAY 362

"In things pertaining to enthusiasm, no man is sane who does not know how to be insane on proper occasions."
HENRY WARD BEECHER

*M*ost people keep their cool too much. Society does not reinforce behavior outside of a very narrow band of emotion. Leaders are especially vulnerable to the perception that people should not bring too much emotion into their work.

Of course, in a crisis situation, the leader who manages to maintain composure and handle any difficulty with calm and rationality is admired. There are times, however, when emotional outbursts are totally acceptable and desirable. People are emotional creatures. Your emotional responses lead the way.

Enthusiastic people laugh. They dance on the tabletops. They sing. They also cry when disappointed. They hug. They live life with a passion that may pass for craziness in the minds of some people, but they get things done.

Show your emotions. Do crazy things once in a while. If you want enthusiastic, spirited individuals on your team, you must show them that you are that way, too, and that you accept the corresponding behaviors from them.

I am a passionate leader and desire that the people on my team also be passionate. I unashamedly demonstrate my emotions and reward the same behaviors in others.

DAY 363

---○---

"To fear is one thing. To let fear grab you by the tail and swing you around is another."
KATHERINE PATERSON

*I*t is normal to have fears. They protect us. They cause chemical reactions that heighten our senses and increase our awareness. They keep us from making decisions that are not in our best interests. Fear, both learned and instinctual, can be our friend as much as it can be our enemy.

The negative side of fear is that it can irrationally keep us from taking action that needs to be taken. By worrying about potential problems, we may not look at the benefits we would have by heading in a certain direction. Keep your fears. It is stupid and dangerous to be fearless. Do not let fears control you. Control them. Use them as your checkpoints to analyze your situation. Once you look at the situation logically, dump the fears and use your rational mind to decide whether action should be taken.

Fears protect me and guide me away from danger, but fear can also be debilitating. Today I will examine what fears are keeping me from taking action, and I will make logical decisions based on the facts.

DAY 364

"My life is my message."
MAHATMA GANDHI

*M*any leaders believe that they are great communicators because they are able to articulate their ideas and visions so that anyone can understand them. While this is one of the key elements of effective communication, it is far from the most important. The most important leadership communication takes place in actions, not in words.

People understand your vision when it is a complete part of your life. You gain people's respect and cooperation when you are doing everything necessary to make the vision part of you. The same is true of values. People honor your values only when you live them completely. When you just declare them the words ring through to nothingness. The most effective way to gain the collaboration of others toward your dreams is to walk the talk. Live the dream. Let your life do the talking for you.

Today I will be aware of inconsistencies between my talk and my walk and take all the steps necessary to ensure that I walk the talk at all times.

DAY 365

"Toleration for error, ambiguity and, above all, diversity, backed by a sense of humor and proportion, are survival necessities as we pack our kit for the amazing trip into the next millennium."
ALVIN AND HEIDI TOFFLER

We are living in the most exciting time in history. Opportunities abound along every step and at every turn. People are searching for leaders with the vision and foresight to carry them into the new world. You are one of the fortunate few chosen by fate to lead others on this exhilarating journey.

You bear a great responsibility. There has never been a time so filled with opportunity yet so fraught with challenges. No one can possibly know all the right answers. The map for the journey is incomplete. It will be a long trip, yet fun. There will be much joy. There will be adventure. Some will make it, and some will not. Keep your attitude of hope and love. Maintain your balance. Travel with integrity. Most of all, be passionate in all your actions. Many people are relying on you to lead them safely on this fantastic adventure into the future.

I am excited to be a leader during the most exciting time in human history. My passion, vision, skills, and abilities assure a safe journey to all who travel the path with me.

About the Author

Donald Luce is president of Cornerstone Learning Systems in San Francisco, California. He is one of today's leading consultants and trainers in leadership and sales development. His clients include many from the Fortune 500 list, as well as small and midsize businesses in today's fastest-growing industries.

Luce has traveled extensively throughout North and South America and Asia, bringing the message that more positive, principled, and directed leadership skills will increase productivity and profit in all companies. He has been involved in international and domestic marketing and management for more than fifteen years.

He lives in San Francisco with his wife and daughter.

You may contact the author at:

CORNERSTONE LEARNING SYSTEMS
21 Columbus Avenue
Suite 214
San Francisco, CA 94111-2101

Telephone: (415) 398-1500
Fax: (415) 398-1554
E-mail: Cornerst1@aol.com